T0150351

# DEAR BABA

*Dear Baba: A Story Through Letters*

ISBN: 978-1-60801-161-2

Cover and Book Design by Alex Dimeff

Photos courtesy of Maryam Rafiee unless otherwise noted.

**UNO PRESS**
unopress.org

# DEAR BABA
a story through letters

## BY MARYAM RAFIEE

ADAM BRAVER, SERIES EDITOR
AND HANNAH LITTLE, ASSISTANT EDITOR

UNO PRESS

# FOREWORD

As with most projects, this one started with an aside. A passing reference. It was in the spring of 2016, and I was in a classroom with a group of students engaged with the Scholars at Risk Student Advocacy Seminar having a Skype conversation with Maryam Rafiee. We were in the state of Rhode Island. She was in the province of Ontario. It was a monthly meeting. The students worked as case minders on behalf of Maryam's father, Professor Mohammad Hossein Rafiee, an Iranian chemistry professor who over the course of his life had dared to raise questions about political issues in his country. At the time of our involvement with him, Professor Rafiee, a political prisoner at age 71, was sitting in the notorious Evin Prison in Iran. Beyond pressing the issues of free expression and the seemingly systemic refraction of the space for open ideas and dialogue, there also were serious concerns about Professor Rafiee's health and his inability to receive the proper treatment in prison.

In a way, the work of the students had migrated from a focus on principles and justice to one that simply was humanitarian.

We looked forward to the meetings with Maryam. Initially, they were formal. Updates on her father's legal situation. Updates on his health. Confirming information the students were gathering. Ensuring that any narrative developed by the students was consistent with the facts, as well as being sensitive to the concerns facing the Rafiee family.

Like most relationships, the more time we spent meeting via Skype throughout the year, the more comfortable we became with each other, and the more comfortable we became with each other, the more the meetings expanded from the role of a briefing and into the congenial comfort of conversation. We learned of Maryam's own career and her background in the sciences. We got glimpses into what her life was like prior to her father's most recent incarceration and how becoming one of her father's chief advocates from abroad (in a very public fashion) had affected her sense of self—including facing the reality that she may never be able to return to Iran. And thus we became partners, and out of that partnership did the story of her letters arise.

She brought them up during one of the virtual discussions, an idea among many ideas for ways to get out more information about her father that would further humanize him in the eyes of people who may have seen him only as a representation. When she mentioned the letters she had written as a teenager to her then jailed father, the students jumped all over it. They wanted to read them! She said she would send one that could be shared on social media, but she cautioned the translation was rough. The students said they would help to clean it up. Once the first letter showed in up our inbox, needless to say, everyone was so blown away by it that they asked for more.

I think Maryam was suspicious. I think she thought we were being nice. Polite. But in fact, we couldn't wait to read more. And she had more. A lot more. An entire collection that, when taken together, turned out to read like a coming-of-age narrative in a time of political turmoil.

The Broken Silence Series strives to show the human side of the daily risks that thinkers face for their ideas. Exploring a variety of cultures and political systems, the books aim to convey what it means to question the dominant power, to fight for the freedom to think, and to endure the consequences of engaging in the just and honest life of ideas from the powerful who are most threatened by such a way of life.

*Dear Baba* is just that sort of book.

While many students in the Scholars at Risk Student Advocacy Seminar contributed to helping Maryam smooth out her translations into English, a special mention is needed for Hannah Little, the assistant editor of this book. She not only paid attention to the nuance of the language, but she also was invaluable in seeing the big picture, voicing concerns and opinions about the narrative flow of the letters, and always advocating for Maryam's intentions.

We are so proud to have *Dear Baba* as part of the Broken Silence Series. Through its epistolary journey, we are reminded that the struggles of conscience are timeless, that most issues that initially seem obvious in fact are quite complex, and that a certain form of vigilance always is required, lest we find ourselves slipping backward in our comfort or distraction of the moment. And yet, at its most basic level, *Dear Baba* also reminds us of the joy and confusion of coming of age and the love of family.

—Adam Braver,
Broken Silence Series Editor
Edgewood,
Rhode Island
November 2018

# INTRODUCTION

I was at the Toronto Amnesty International rally in support of political prisoners in Iran. I was standing in front of the crowd, holding my father's photo in my left hand and talking about his situation at Evin Prison in Tehran.

"My father will be 72 years old next month," I told the crowd. Then I paused and looked at his photo. When I raised my head to continue my sentence, I couldn't. I choked up and couldn't get the words out. I was hardly able to compose myself to say, "He suffers from poor health. However, he is being denied sufficient medical care."

In just those few seconds as I looked at his photo, these questions beset me: Why should my father be in prison because of his thoughts? Why should my mother, brother, and I be put through this much suffering and pain due to his detention? When will this cycle of threat, arrest, and detention end?

My father was arrested in June 2015 in the midst of nuclear negotiations between Iran and the world powers. He was among the few scholars inside the country who publicly supported the negotiations and encouraged the moderate government to reach a deal. However, his writings were not being tolerated by the hardliners. He was tried privately, without a jury, and sentenced to six years in prison with charges of "being a member of the *Melli-Mazhabi* Coalition" and "spreading propaganda against the State." This was not the first time that his freedom of speech was violated, though.

It was in March of 2001, a few days before the Persian New Year (*Nowruz*), that my father was arrested along with his friends when Revolutionary Court agents raided their meeting. He was imprisoned for six months, mostly in solitary confinement, under tremendous pressure to accept the absurd charges against himself.

I was a teenaged girl at the time and carrying strong emotions, like all girls at this age. My feelings and reactions to his arrest were different and even contradictory with the passage of time. In the beginning, I was excited about the new and unique experiences that this situation had brought to me, such as visiting Parliament or participating in a press conference. But very soon I faced the bitter side; I experienced an unbearable pain and anguish because I couldn't talk to my father or visit him. Knowing the reality that we didn't have the power to end this unjust situation made me anxious and even angry. The only way I was able to unburden these feelings was by writing. Almost every night, I secluded myself in my room and wrote a letter to my father about the happenings at home, school, and around the country, as well as my activities, dreams, and feelings – almost everything.

My father was being detained in an undisclosed prison without access to his lawyer or any kind of news. Except for some short phone calls and a few visits under supervision, we may as well have had no contact with him. This situation motivated me more to document every piece of news and happenings that he missed during his detention. In addition to writing, I bought a bunch of newspapers every day and made an archive of the news and articles related to his arrest and also recorded all the news and statements broadcasted on national TV.

On the first night of his freedom, I gave him all the letters. He didn't expected that. I clearly recall his face, how he was surprised by them. He read the letters in a day or two and for days and months afterwards, he insisted I publish them publicly. I hesitated, though. He thought the letters illustrated the pro-democracy activities of certain people in that specific period of Iran and that I should tell others about them. I didn't think like him. My only answer to his insistence was: "I wrote them for you, Baba. These are private. I don't want others to read them."

But, after fifteen years, when I looked at my father's photo at the Amnesty International rally and those questions beset me, an idea struck my mind: it's time to tell my story to the world. I thought to myself that this situation would not change if I stayed silent about what happened then and what is happening now to my family. Silence just helps oppression and injustice remain strong and this is what I am trying to avoid.

That night, I read over the letters for the first time in years. It was tough. The old wounds reopened. I burst into tears many times, recalling the heartbreaking events of the time. The suffering and pain became so intense that there was a moment when I came close to changing my mind and leaving the letters aside like I had for the last fifteen years. But I didn't. This hope that by telling my story, I might help to prevent another father from being arrested due to his ideas and prevent another daughter from suffering due to her father's detention, motivated me to continue.

When I finished reading, I was more determined to publish them than ever. My father was right. People should know this story. They should know that detaining him was not fair, neither then nor now. But specifically, I want those who arrested him to read these letters. I want them to know that not only did they imprison my father, but they imprisoned me, my brother, and my mother as well. Not only did they violate his rights, but they violated ours, too. Not only did they hurt him, but they hurt us, too. I want them to read my letters and know what they did to me as a child, as a teenaged girl. Maybe then they will stop doing this to other children.

I narrate a story through my letters, a story of courageous women, men, and children who struggled for freedom and never lost hope. I hope this account encourages other people who have gone through similar or more difficult ordeals to write about their experiences. Injustice must be stopped at some point, and this will never happen unless we all break our silence.

# MARCH

*Sunday, 11 March, 2001*
*Midnight*

Dear Baba Hossein,

It was 8:30 in the evening when we found out that Mr. Basteh-negar's[1] house was raided by the Revolutionary Court agents and all of you were arrested. Because Maman was not at home, Mohammad[2] walked to Mr. Basteh-negar's house in order to get some news and I answered the non-stop phone calls; many already had heard of the news and were calling for updates.

It was an hour after Mohammad had left when I started to worry about him. He was late and he didn't call either, so cousin Ali and I decided to go find him. As soon as our car entered the alley and stopped in front of Mr. Basteh-negar's house, several agents came out of the house and surrounded the car. They all looked alike to me, with their similar clothes and stubbly beards. They were not in uniform but all of them wore a loose, long, untucked shirt over their slack pants.

One of the agents asked Ali, "Who are you? What are you doing here?" Ali said that he is coming after his cousin,

---

1       A member of *Melli-Mazhabi* Coalition, a pro-democracy political coalition that came together to contest the 2000 parliamentary elections in Iran.
2       My older brother.

Mohammad. He didn't mention that his father—Uncle Reza—is also among the arrestees.

"Go back home," the agent said.

I stretched my head out of the car window and asked another agent standing close to me, "Is my brother inside?"

He yelled, "Go back home. We will send him back later." We didn't have the choice or power to confront them, so we returned home.

Mohammad finally came back an hour later. Don't worry, Baba, he is fine. They didn't do anything to him. They kept him in the basement and asked him few questions, such as, "Who are you? Why do you come here?" and so on… After the questions, they let him go.

When Maman came home, she immediately called Mr. Abtahi, the president's chief of staff, and explained the situation so that he may inform President Khatami.

Baba, I'm sorry! My mind is so muddled right now. I can't focus on my writing. Maman is tearing up her diaries and writings in her room. She says our home may be raided too and she doesn't want them to take her personal notes. I don't want them to, either. Is Maman right? Do you think they will raid our home, too?

Maman is going to the Revolutionary Court tomorrow, along with the families of the other arrestees. There were twenty of you arrested at tonight's meeting, including you and Uncle Reza.

Nobody knows what is happening or why!

By the way, I have a confession to make. Please don't be upset when you reach this part of my letter. I really don't want to hide any of my feelings, so I shall say that since I've heard of your arrest, I have had a strange feeling. It's a mixture of excitement and anxiety. It's a funny sensation, isn't it? I've never had one quite like this before; it keeps me up tonight. I wish I knew where you are and what you are doing now.

Love you and goodnight.

*Monday, 12 March, 2001*
*11:25 pm*

Maman and others went to the Revolutionary Court this morning. She brought your allergy medicine and some clothes. They took your medicine but did not accept your clothes. I hope you've received it by now. She also went to Parliament in the evening to meet some of the Reformist MPs.[3]

I couldn't move from the phone today. Many people called me asking for news. But still, everything is a mystery to all of us — even the MPs don't know what has happened and why you were arrested!!

Baba! You wouldn't believe what we heard on TV tonight! Last night's arrest was covered on the news and Mr. Mobasheri, Head of the Revolutionary Court, said in an interview that they arrested a group who were "plotting to overthrow the State"! I can't imagine this! Where is this coming from? Everyone is so shocked and worried, since this is a really huge and heavy accusation against you.

Tomorrow, all the families are supposed to go to the Revolutionary Court again, and I want to go, too. I am really excited to see what it looks like.

Good night.

---

3    Members of Parliament.

*Tuesday, 13 March, 2001*
*Midnight*


Hello Baba,

This morning, around 1:00 a.m., nine of your comrades were released. After last night's news, this is a good sign. We now know that you are all in solitary confinement, but no one knows where.

The families of those arrested were in front of the Revolutionary Court this morning at 10:30. Maman and I also went. We got a body search when we wanted to go inside the building. After the inspection, we came to a crowded reception hall with rows of benches and desks up front. I even saw some prisoners in handcuffs and shackles.

In order to go upstairs where the Court's various branches are, people are required to stand in a long line. When their turn comes, an agent asks which branch they are going to. He then may or may not call the branch. If you get permission to go to the branch, he takes your ID and issues a pass for you. Without this pass paper, you cannot access to the branch.

However, for us it was different. When we walked into the hall it seemed that they knew us, so we didn't have to stand in the line. One of the agents called Branch 26 and then told us that the deputy of that branch is coming down now. Yesterday he had come down to talk with the families and had introduced himself as Seyed Majid, without mentioning his family name! I was really eager to see him, as everyone talked about him after yesterday's meeting.

After couple of minutes, Seyed Majid came down. He seemed middle aged, a little bit chubby, and short with a messy, black beard. He wore a loose-fitting long sleeved shirt that was untucked, the bottom hem falling over his pants. He stood in the middle of the hall and loudly said, "Talk one by one!"

Mrs. Rajaee[4] asked, "How is Mr. Rajaee's situation?"

---

4        Wife of one of the arrestees.

"A temporary detention order is issued for a month-long term," Seyed Majid answered. He added, "And no meeting is allowed."

We asked one by one about those of you who were still detained and the answer for all was the same. He did not respond to our questions as to where the detainees were being held and just said, "In a detention center under the supervision of the Prisons Organization."

One of the women said, "We are worried about them" (or something like this), and suddenly, Seyed Majid's voice turned rough at this unified opposition.

"*Do not speak on others' behalf!!*" he yelled.

Another woman in the crowd raised her voice: "Why do you want to separate us? We are all *Melli-Mazhabi* members' families. You arrested them all together and now you should answer us all together."

Then it became chaotic. Maman was yelling at him and so were others. He was not the same man who came down confidently just few minutes ago; now he was surrounded by twelve angry, determined women who were desperately demanding information about their husbands. I don't think anybody wants to be in his situation, don't you agree with me, Baba?

Seyed Majid tried hard to hide his anxiety under his nervous laughs. And I just kept still and observed the situation.

After this inconclusive discussion at the Revolutionary Court, the women decided to go to Parliament and meet some of the MPs. I don't know if you have seen the new Parliament before or not? For me it was the first time. The exterior of the building was still undergoing construction and so there was dust and dirt surrounding it everywhere.

We arrived just as the representatives were leaving Parliament in their cars. We stood in front of the parking lot's gate. Some of them stopped and got out of their cars when they noticed us. Mr. Bourghani[5] got out of his Renault and in a very friendly and

---

5      A Reformist MP (2000-2004).

sympathetic manner, he told Maman that "we are doing everything in our power to solve this issue." He said that chairman of the Parliament, Mr. Karoubi, talked with The Supreme Leader and chief of the judiciary for four-to-five hours last night regarding this arrest and this heavy accusation. He also mentioned that about one hundred and fifty-two representatives signed a letter of support today in Parliament, objecting to the arrest of *Melli-Mazhabi* Coalition members.

While the women were talking to some other Reformist representatives, I noticed the ordinary people who were standing outside the parking lot; just like us, they were waiting for their representatives. They ran after their cars, begging for a signature on their letters, hoping that some intervention by the representatives would help resolve whatever issue they may have had. These were the people who voted for them and chose them to be in Parliament and now their representatives came out in their flashy Peugeot Persias and ignored them! Ah! This is not what I envisioned Parliament to be like.

Baba! This is perhaps the first and last time that I have experienced all these new adventures and I am so excited about them. Please overlook my excitement. I know I should be upset and worried about your situation. I do, I really do. But I am excited, too, and I don't want to hide it.

I am exhausted and too sleepy! It was a long day.

Good night!

*Thursday, 15 March, 2001*
*11:40 pm*

Dear Baba Hossein,
We haven't heard anything from you for *four days*. Why don't you call us?
This morning, all the families were at the Revolutionary Court again. Seyed Majid came down to issue the passes in order allow us to go to Branch 26 and meet the judge who is called Haddad.[6] When Maman gave him her ID, Seyed Majid said, "You should be accountable for your words the other morning; I recorded your insults!" What? Maman didn't insult anybody. She'd just said that you've been unlawfully arrested and should be released! Maman told him firmly and calmly, "No problem. I'll talk to the judge."

You know, Baba, I think Seyed Majid doesn't know Maman; otherwise, he would never threaten her like this.

Because just one member of each family is allowed to go upstairs, I stayed alone in the hall. I killed time watching the people who came in and out of the Court. Men, women, young, old, even children. Each had their unique story. I found this to be kind of sad.

You know, Baba, the most heartbreaking scenes for me were those moments when the front desk agents yelled at these desperate people: "You can't go upstairs... Don't insist... Get out!" They would turn around, walk to the exit, and try to avoid making any eye contact with the crowd.

I hate that damn court. What are you doing there, Baba? You don't belong in that place!!

Finally, after two hours, Maman and the other women came down. It was 1:15 and the Court was going to be closed very soon. Judge Haddad apologized to Maman about Seyed Majid's behavior. He even accepted Maman's request to send you a short

---

6     Hassan Zareh Dehnavi, known as Judge Haddad, was the head of Branch 26 of the Revolutionary Court and in charge of the *Mel-li-Mazhabi* Coalition arrest.

note. She asked you if you have received your antihistamine pills and what she should do with *Chemistry & Development* magazine.[7] Hopefully you can answer.

As to the larger issue, Judge Haddad didn't say anything more than what we already knew. He repeated that you are all subjected to a temporary arrest for interrogation. The only new thing was that Uncle Reza was supposed to be released last night, but due to some issues (Haddad didn't mention what kind of issues!), they decided to keep him.

In the afternoon, Maman and other families of arrestees met Mr. Karroubi, Chairman of the Parliament, in his office in Saad Abad. He told them that he is trying hard to get you released by *Nowruz*.[8] Hopefully you will!

Love you.

---

7       The Magazine which Baba ran (April 2000 – March 2001).

8       *Nowruz* is the Persian New Year, which is celebrated on the first day of spring (21 March).

*Saturday, 17 March, 2001*

It's one hour after midnight and I couldn't sleep because of my excitement. I still can't believe you called. It was 8:00 in the evening and I was alone at home. When I picked up the phone and heard your voice, I was too flustered to say anything.

All the words I had rehearsed over and over in my mind during the last few days were gone. My lips were glued together. I just asked, "How are you?" and you answered, "Don't be worried, I am fine." Your voice was too faint, as if it came from bottom of a well. However, I feel that you are fine. Did our conversation last for even a minute? You said, "I gotta go," and then it was goodbye. That's it.

Baba dear! I wanted to give you hope and power, but I didn't use this opportunity. I wanted to tell you that I am proud of you, no matter what happens. I wanted to tell you to stay strong and be patient. But I said none of that, and I am so angry at myself. Hopefully, you sensed what I really meant to say.

Another exciting piece of news is that we had a press conference this morning at one of the *Melli-Mazhabi* member's office. Mrs. Basteh-negar and three other wives of the arrestees represented the families at the press conference.

At the end of the room, they sat at a long desk with their backs to the windows, facing the journalists who were very busy taking photos, writing in notebooks, and recording their voices. Many reporters attended, mostly from Reformist newspapers.

One of the journalists asked Mrs. Basteh-negar about the procedure of your arrest at her house. She explained that on last Sunday, at around 5 p.m., a number of agents from the Revolutionary Court entered the house after presenting a search warrant to Mr. Basteh-negar. At the beginning, the agents told everyone that they were just coming for a house inspection, and that no one could leave before they were done. She mentioned that the agents were in constant contact with their headquarters by phone — giving information and receiving orders. She said,

"This situation lasted 'til 9:00, when finally they told everyone in the meeting that they were detained under the command of the Revolutionary Court."

Other questions were about your actual situation in the prison, the accusations you are facing, and the demands of the families. The families' representatives answered the reporters' questions and firmly objected to the accusations against you. They said there's no evidence that you are "subversive" and "plotting to overthrow the state." Such talk is unacceptable to the families.

The press conference was really awesome. It was like you were very famous and important people, the kind that everyone likes to know about in the news. I've seen press conferences before on TV, but this was the first real press conference I've ever attended – and, of course, the most important. I am so excited to see what they write tomorrow in the papers.

Maman didn't come to the conference; instead, she'd gone to the Revolutionary Court to see if you answered the questions she had sent to you the other day. And guess what? *Yes yes yes.* You wrote a short letter to Maman on the back of her note. You don't know how happy and reassured your handwriting makes us feel.

You wrote that we shouldn't be worried and that "everything's gonna be okay." Baba, you said that Mohammad and I should focus on our studies. I know this might disappoint you, but studying is actually the last thing I've been worried about these days. Poor Mohammad! He has to study for the university entrance exam, and I have no idea how he concentrates on his studies!! Since your arrest, I have had a lot of adventures and new experiences, all of which have caused and encouraged me to turn my back on boring lessons and run away to experience and learn new things. Baba, you don't object, do you?

Regarding the Chemistry and Development magazine, you told Maman that you can't decide about its future at this point and asked that she just pay your secretary's salary. But the really good news: you received your allergy medicine.

Baba! It was a short letter but it is a big comfort for us. Thank you.

Good night.

P.S. God, please give my father the power to endure this situation. Amen.

*Sunday, 18 March, 2001*
*11:30 pm*

Dear Baba Hossein,

The good news is that Uncle Reza and one other arrestee called their homes today, and they are fine. Hopefully others will call too and ease their families' worries.

The bad news is that the Revolutionary Court released a statement today that has very unjustly condemned you. The 2:00 news on Channel One broadcasted the news. The statement read that the "*Melli-Mazhabi* Coalition is an illegal group, its activities are currently under court review, and the documents of its subversive activities will be revealed soon."

I was eating lunch when I heard the news headlines and I lost my appetite right away. *You are in the headlines*, I first thought. And then I realized, *Oops, something is going wrong!*

I called Maman and Mohammad and started recording the news. We were all staring at the TV, listening carefully to the presenter reading the statement.

Baba, this statement is very harsh, hostile, and merciless. It gives us the feeling that the Court has already made its decision before interrogations take place and a trial is held. All the families are in shock, as this statement clearly indicates that your accusation is serious and you won't be released very soon.

In the evening, all the families were at Mr. Emrani's[9] house to decide how we will celebrate *Nowruz*. It's not certain yet, but we will most likely gather in front of Evin Prison to celebrate the New Year there. We chose Evin symbolically, as we don't know where you are detained. Of course, if we find out your place of detention, then we'll gather there to be as close as we can to you. Just three days left. I can't believe you won't be with us for this *Nowruz*!

Take care, Baba dear!

---

9    A member of the *Melli-Mazhabi* Coalition.

*Monday, 19 March, 2001*
*Midnight*


My Dearest Baba,

I haven't seen you for a week. I can't believe how quickly the time has passed. I didn't think it would become this serious. I figured you'd be released in the first two or three days, but nothing is as I would wish it to be.

Guess what I did today in the Tajrish Bazaar? You'll be proud of me. Tara[10] and I went to the bazaar for shopping, but even more so for watching the vitality and joy that spring brings to the city. Huge crowds of people were doing their last-minute New Year's shopping. The bazaar was really crazy. People were browsing, bargaining, and shopping from stalls. We could barely squeeze through the crowd into the shops. Sidewalks were full of hawkers who laid their goods and products on the ground, all surrounded by people.

By chance, we met a hawker who was selling musical instruments. Not many people were around him, which is not a surprise. We went closer to take a look at the instruments. Tara suggested that I could do something that would be crazy in that crowd and I accepted. I think you've guessed already what I did, haven't you? Yes, I picked up a *Daf* from his instruments and started playing the drum. For just a second, all the noises around us stopped after my fingers tapped the goatskin and the metal rings started dancing in the air. I closed my eyes to concentrate on the rhythm, but more because I was too shy to look into peoples' eyes. This was the first time I played in open air for a huge, unknown audience. When I finished my street performance, the big crowd around us started applauding and saying, "Well done . . . That's awesome! . . . Play again!" I put the *Daf* back, grabbed Tara's hand, and ran away, disappearing into the crowd. When we were far enough away, we stopped running and started laughing; you know, those non-stop laughs we do all the time. It was so much fun.

---

10      My close friend.

Thank you, Baba, a thousand times, thanks for supporting me in pursuing my wishes. Several years ago, when I told you that I wanted to play *Daf,* you bought me one and took me to the music class every week. In those days, Mohammad and I had to put our instruments in your car's trunk to hide them from the *Basij's*[11] inspections on the streets. Can you believe that today, not only can the instruments be carried on the street, but I can also play freely without any fear?

Many changes have occurred, and these changes are due to your work and the work of people like you who attempt to improve the situation in Iran.

In what seems like just the last few moments, spring has come finally to our home. Today, Maman and I finally did the house-cleaning and set the *Haft Seen.*[12] I set it on a table by the entry to our house; it catches the eye as soon as the door is opened. I framed a photo of you that I found in one of your old photo albums and put it on the table. Maman said it doesn't look like you at your actual age! It's kind of true. The photo is dated back to the 70's, when you were studying in America. But I like it, as, in that photo, you were more handsome (and still with hair). I also wrote you a postcard that I bought today in the bazaar. It has a picture of a white dove of peace with an olive branch. I put it on the table with the wish that peace will come back to our home again.

The exact time of vernal equinox will be 5 p.m. tomorrow. I don't know if you'll be released or not? Seems not… But, still, I'm thinking of you with all my heart.

Baba, although many times I had felt that I wanted to have a normal family like my friends did, and I nagged you because you had always been busy with your reading, writing, and meetings, you must know that I am proud of you. If you come back home, you will never hear me complain again. I swear.

Goodbye 'til New Year.

---

11      The *Basij* militia is an Iranian force organized by the Islamic Revolutionary Guards Corps.
12      *Haft Seen* is a tabletop arrangement of seven symbolic items traditionally displayed at *Nowruz*.

*Tuesday, 20 March, 2001*
*Midnight*

Dear Baba Hossein,
*Happy New Year!*
This is the first *Nowruz* that you're not with us. You are missed so badly.

What did you do for the New Year? Did they tell you that it's time? Did they give you sweet pastries?

I think your cell is too gloomy and dreary to let you feel the coming of spring and the New Year. How could a person celebrate the New Year alone in solitary confinement? I couldn't imagine how torturous and painful that must have been!!

If you are detained in Evin, I should tell you that we were there for the New Year, just a few meters from you. All the families gathered in front of Evin Prison before 5:00. We set the *Haf Seen* on the ground and gathered around it. Many other friends and relatives had come, too. It was such a big gathering.

Baba, you wouldn't believe it, but the passing cars stopped and asked the reason for our gathering. When we explained, they sympathized with us and said they wished you would be released soon. Some of them even got out of their cars and joined us.

Just minutes before 5:00, we started praying for you around our *Haft Seen*. Tears silently rolled down many faces, but everyone remained very calm and still while whispering a prayer. It was a spiritual atmosphere. And then the clock-hand ticked and stopped at five. We all rejoiced, kissed, and embraced each other. It was a different start for a New Year. Grief and joy tied together!

After exchanging *Nowruz* greetings, some other girls and I distributed pastries among the people and passing cars. Many journalists had come, too. They took photos and interviewed everyone. At the beginning, there weren't any security agents around, but after a while they came and tried to scatter the crowd.

Later, we went to Aunt Mali's house for New Year's dinner. We ate a very delicious *Sabzi Polo Mahi*.[13] What did you eat?

Baba! Many people called, except you. Every time the phone rang, I ran to it, telling myself, "this is Baba, this is Baba." But I was wrong every time. They wouldn't even let you call us for a simple *Nowruz* greeting. That is not fair at all.

I miss you!

P.S. Everyone is sleeping, but I couldn't. I am sitting now at our *Haft Seen* table and looking at your picture and a green candle, which I lit in remembrance of your green eyes with the hope that no one takes their brightness away. Although, I believe no one would be able to do so. Love you, Baba!

---

13      Herbed rice with fish is the traditional Iranian New Year's meal.

*Wednesday, 21 March, 2001*

Hello Baba,

It's two hours after midnight and I am tired to death. We had visitors from 8:00 in the morning 'til two hours ago. I have never seen that many people come into our house in one day.

On the first day of *Nowruz*, typically younger people visit the elders; however, because of your arrest it seems nobody cares about traditions. Whoever you can think of came here today for *Nowruz* greetings—old and young, relatives, neighbors, friends, and even many people whose names I did not know.

Our home constantly went from full of people, to empty, to full again. I would be standing in front of the door to welcome a group of guests and at the same time saying goodbye to another. Can you believe I still didn't have enough time to sit or talk with anyone?

I had many emotional moments today; if I'd had time, I would've burst into tears. Tears of joy, not sadness. All these people, instead of spending their time with their families on the first day of the New Year, came here to show their sympathy, support, and unity. To tell us that we are not alone through this tough time. All this kindness and support was beyond my expectation.

Baba, I wish you could know how much people care about you and how much they respect you. The people who I barely knew held me tightly in their arms and told me, "You should proud of your Baba; he is a respectful man." And I am, I really am.

*Baba, I am proud of being your daughter.*

Good night!

*Saturday, 24 March, 2001*
*One and half hours after midnight*

You know what Aunt Mahin said few days ago about our home? "It's like the Ministry of Foreign Affairs!" she said. "Non-stop phone calls! Non-stop visitors!"

I have no clue about the Ministry of Foreign Affairs, but I agree with her point about the calls and visitors. Our home is so busy these days; I'm thinking that you were actually arrested at a good time of the year, because if it happened at any other time apart from the New Year holidays, I would definitely have trouble keeping up with my lessons. Please don't be upset, Baba! I don't mean it. I'm just trying to see the glass as half full.

Unlike me, Mohammad is studying hard. He keeps his room's door shut and focuses on his studies. At least, I guess so! I don't know what goes through his mind. You know he is exactly the opposite of me! He doesn't show reactions to anything, especially these days!!

Some of your colleagues at the university were here this morning. They prepared a draft of an appeal letter to President Khatami to support the arrested university professors, including you, Uncle Reza, Dr. Maleki, and Dr. Peyman. In the letter, they express their concern regarding your arrest, your detention in an unknown prison, and your solitary confinement. They also request for the president to do everything in his power to assure that your legal rights are respected. After the holidays, the letter will be circulated among academics to gather their signatures. You see, Baba, everyone is supporting you.

Last night, the families also gathered here for making a decision on our next steps. The women think that we shouldn't keep silent about you, especially after that unjust statement made by the Revolutionary Court. So, they decided to write a letter to the UN Human Rights Commissioner regarding your situation.

Baba, have I told you how much calmer I feel when I am writing to you? Particularly at night, when I am writing under the reading lamp in my room—surrounded by your huge bookshelves —I feel refuged by your books and the knowledge of somehow being surrounded by all their writers. Feels good!

Despite that, I think you need to organize your bookshelves after your release. Just look how you arranged the books! The shelves are clogged with tons of books, with some that line up vertically, some that stack horizontally on top of another vertical stack, and some placed behind the others. You just crammed the books wherever you found a spot. I wonder how you would find them?!

I love you, but please, no more books, Baba!

*Monday, 26 March, 2001*
*11:15 am*


Dear Baba Hossein,

I'm sorry that I didn't write you last night. I fell asleep early and I totally forgot to write.

Yesterday morning, Maman went to the Revolutionary Court after a week without any news from you. She complained to them that we haven't heard from you since the New Year and got angry at them. She left the Court with no updates about you. However, this didn't end the day. Maman's anger at the Court seemed to be effective, in that they let you call home. When you phoned us at 10:00 last night, it seemed that you were fine. You told me, "I owe you a New Year's present. I'll give it to you with its interest." And then you laughed. You can't imagine how much I've missed your laugh.

Yesterday afternoon, the families gathered at Dr. Peyman's house. They wrote and signed some letters to the authorities. You know, Baba, these women are so good at advocacy for their husbands. They are working hard to prove that you are innocent.

The families take their meetings very seriously. Every time, a chairwoman is chosen to preside over the meeting. She makes sure everyone has a turn to talk, and she keeps the time. The meetings begin with them sharing news relating to those detained, which can vary from a phone call with one of their husbands to visiting a Member of Parliament or any other authority. Then, if a letter is supposed to be signed, someone will read it aloud and others will give their comments. If no editing is needed, it is signed and ready to send; otherwise, it's kept for revising.

The meeting will then continue with the presentation of new ideas and suggestions. Anyone who has a suggestion about writing a letter to someone and/or an organization, or taking a certain action, is called to speak up. After a discussion, they'll vote on the new action, which only can be approved with more than two-thirds of the vote. At the end of the meeting, volunteers are chosen to work on the letters or the minutes for the next meeting.

You see, Baba, how professional and organized we are fighting for your rights.

P.S. Baba, I miss you so much. I can't sleep tonight. I feel a heaviness in my heart because of this cruel and unjust world. You haven't done anything wrong, and yet they keep you in prison, despite your innocence. I feel that we are so oppressed. But you know, as long as we comply with the wishes of tyrants, there never will be any changes. We must confront and resist this oppression. We must defend our rights and show them that we don't want to be oppressed. Don't you agree with me? Please be strong.

*Tuesday, 27 March, 2001*
*One hour after midnight*


I will start my letter with good news; Dr. Peyman had a visit with his family at the Revolutionary Court. That's a good sign. It means, they might give us a visiting time, too. *Wow!* It would be great if I could visit you! But I want your unconditional release; there shouldn't be any preconditions for releasing an innocent person, should there?

And now, I impatiently want to tell you about my new decision. I've decided to become the Secretary General of the United Nations, just like Mr. Kofi Annan. Actually, I've been thinking about it for a long time, and I am pleased to reveal my plan to you – the first person to know. It first occurred me when I attended the "Hello Children of the Earth!" conference last year. Do you remember that?

I had a controversial idea for the conference. At first, I'd hesitated to work on it; however, your encouragement made me decide to go for it. I hope you are not being interrogated for my contribution to that conference.

Writing a letter to Chelsea Clinton, daughter of the United States President, is still a huge taboo in this country, but still I did it! Baba, if they ask about my letter, tell them that your daughter just wrote about our history, culture, and religion in order to show that we are a very peaceful nation. And please emphasize that *she hates war* and wants to solve the problems through negotiations. I just wrote according to what the conference was about: "Dialogue Among Civilizations."

Oh, now I just remembered that I insisted that you translate my letter and send it to the White House. I had completely forgotten that part. However, I am sure that my letter didn't even get out of the post office, let alone getting to the USA. Just imagine the flustered post officer when he read the address on the envelope: *"White House!"* He probably delivered it to the intelligence agents right away. Do you think they've read my letter? I think that just like the conference organizers, the intelligence agents might have appreciated it; otherwise, they would have come after me by now.

Had I told you that the first time I met the conference organizers, one of them introduced me to the others as *the girl who wrote a letter to Clinton's daughter*? I was supposed to be chosen as one of the presenters, and I was meant to be a member of the symbolic management committee. I even started all the training and practice sessions. But suddenly, and without any explanation, they replaced me with someone who hadn't even participated in a single one of those sessions! They might have been cautious about the consequences of choosing me for those roles, as I was the girl who started a dialogue with the *"Big Enemy."* It was so disappointing! At the time, I didn't tell you anything about this because my pride had been broken and, at that point, I didn't even want to attend the conference anymore.

Maman, with her maternal feelings (I guess), found out that I was upset. She told me: "These things happen to all those who try to swim against the current. If you believe in what you've done, then be strong, attend the conference, and share your idea with other children. It doesn't matter if you are a presenter or a normal attendee, but it would matter if you chose to be silent and step back."

She was right. The conference experience ended up being wonderful. I found out that many children in this country, just like me, prefer dialogue rather than hatred and enmity. After the conference, this caused me to think more about the concept of "Dialogue Among Civilizations." I have thought of many questions but have not found satisfying answers for them. Why is there so much war and violence in the world? Why do some people think they are superior to others? Why do some powers want hegemony over the entire world? Every time I see innocent people killed, it makes me sick. I want to stop this. I think people of different countries need to talk more with each other and share their cultures and beliefs. We might be different in language and color, but we are all human and deserve to live in peace. Don't we, Baba?

However, to resume my original point, I've decided to become the Secretary General of the United Nations to stop the wars around the world and to spread peace. I am not sure this position has that much power and, according to my (aforementioned) experience, I'm aware that there would be a lot of obstacles and disappointments on my way. But I am willing to go for it. Where there's a will, there's a way. What do you think, dear Dr. Rafiee?

A very warm goodnight from the future Secretary General of the UN.

*Wednesday, 28 March, 2001*
*One hour after midnight*

Hello Baba,

My mind is so playful tonight. It won't let me sleep. It's because of the film I watched in the evening, *Scabies,* directed by Abolfazl Jalili. Have you seen it before?

It's about the painful lives of young offenders who are serving time in a reformatory before the Revolution. They suffer from poor hygiene and nutrition, not to mention the harsh treatment of officers. I have no clue about the current condition of reformatories, but hopefully they have been improved over these past twenty years.

A unique scene of the film sticks in my head and won't go away: the children are squatting on the ground, leaning against a wall in the yard, and roughly scrubbing their heads against it while the prison agent is yelling at them, "Scrub harder! Scrub harder!" You know why they had to do that? It was for removing the head lice!!

Whenever I close my eyes, this scene plays in front of me. But instead of the children, I see all of you squatting in the prison yard and scrubbing your heads. And Seyed Majid is yelling at you, walking back and forth in front of you and moving his hand up and down: "Scrub harder, Rafiee… You should be more serious, Maleki… Raissi, just do it! I am talking to all of you. Scrub harder!"

You raise your head and say, "Many of us are bald! There is no possibility for head lice! Why should we scrub our heads?"

"No dispute! Everyone should follow the regulations," he says as he pushes your head down. "There is no exception."

*Hahaha…* Sorry, Baba, but it makes me laugh. I know I am too mean. I'll try to shut down my imagination and sleep.

Good night.

*Thursday, 29 March, 2001*
*Midnight*

Have I told you I have been making an archive since your arrest? I buy several newspapers every day, and I read the political pages carefully (something that I barely did before) to find any news regarding you. Then, I cut out the articles or the editorials and glue them separately onto A4 papers. I write the name of the newspaper and publishing date on top of each paper, punch it, and put it in a 3-ring binder. *Voila*, this is my archive!

Tara is here tonight for a sleepover. She is reading my archive now and she looks totally amazed. Every few minutes she raises her head up and tells me, "Good job. You should continue this."

Baba, I can't wait to see your reaction to it. I am sure you will love it, too.

I have bad news again!

Yesterday, the families gathered at Dr. Maleki's house, and they decided to go to the Revolutionary Court to ask for a visiting time. Some of the women went there this morning – Maman wasn't among them. We heard later that a dispute occurred between the families and the Courts' agents. The agents didn't treat them very well. Apparently, they even wanted to punch Mrs. Basteh-negar's face! (I just heard, I wasn't there!) Judge Haddad was probably not at the Court or didn't show up, so the women left there with no results.

This situation is not fair for any of us!

*Friday, 30 March, 2001*
*11:30 pm*

Dear Baba Hossein,

This morning, Maman and I went for a walk in Darakeh.[14] Mrs. Maleki also joined us. She told us more about what had happened yesterday in the Revolutionary Court, but if you don't mind, I really don't want to write about it. Sometimes, I feel all these events and experiences are going far beyond what I can bear, and I don't want to recall them all by writing. I feel we are in a humiliating, offensive, oppressive, and unbearable situation!! Do you feel the same?

I'll try to talk about something else. Tehran is so quiet during the *Nowruz* holiday. It seems that the whole city is in slumber. We really enjoyed the mild breeze and sunshine while walking in the valley. The smell of spring was being carried everywhere by the wind. It was intoxicating and exhilarating—the fresh scent of grass and damp, rain soaked soil mixed with the pleasing scent of jasmine. You want to stay there and just look at the endless blue sky, filled with white puffy clouds, and listen to the sound of the river.

From where we walked in Darakeh, I could see the Evin Prison wall that goes all around the mountain facing us. It seems like such a big prison from outside! Maman says that the Shah built it to detain his opponents and that after the Revolution, it was also used for detaining political prisoners.

Baba, is it disappointing if I say I really want to see what the inside of the prison looks like? Honestly, I do. I should wait 'til we get a visiting time with you. Do you think it will be at Evin Prison, or another one? Many believe that you are in hands of *Sepah*[15] and imprisoned in one of their secret places! But who knows?

When I was looking at the Evin Prison wall, I asked myself, "Is Baba detained there? Can he look at the sky? What is he doing

---

14    A neighborhood north of Tehran.
15    The Islamic Revolutionary Guards Corps (IRGC), commonly known as the *Sepah*, is a branch of Iran's armed forces, founded after the 1979 Iranian Revolution.

exactly, at this moment? Is he thinking about me?" Are you thinking about me, Baba?

It is so difficult to write letters to you without expecting any answers! But I'll do it 'til you get released. I promise.

Good night.

# APRIL

*Monday, 2 April, 2001*
*One and a half hours after midnight*

Hello Baba,

Today was *Sizdah Be-dar*.[16] I can't believe thirteen days have passed already! It was the most awful *Nowruz* holiday I've ever had. I haven't done any of my plans for studying and practicing music. It seems like our life is in limbo since your arrest. It is as though we are waiting for something to happen, but we are not exactly sure what that could be, and we don't have any power to change the situation. We still don't know why you were arrested, why they accused you of being subversive, why they don't tell us where you are detained, why we can't visit you, why you don't call us, and there are so many other "whys"!

Baba, I want to cry...

I am back again. I cried silently into my pillow and now I feel better. I had meant to write a cheerful and nice letter but I don't know why I started like that!

This evening, I watched another film of Abolfazl Jalili's called *Don*. It was about an eight-year-old boy without a birth certificate.

---

16    *Sizdah Be-dar* is an Iranian festival held annually on the thirteenth day of *Nowruz*, during which people spend time picnicking outdoors.

His parents were both drug addicts and they had failed to get him a certificate. So, he had no identity, no education, and no job prospects. But he tried hard to solve his problem and to get a birth certificate for himself.

When I compare my life with his and consider how a little boy has such struggles in his life, but never complains, I feel ashamed of myself. I have everything in my life: I have caring parents, I have a comfortable home and have meals prepared for me, I study in a good school, I have my entertainment, I also have my freedom and independence (something that many girls at my age don't have), as well as many other things that I forget to be grateful for.

I'm sorry now for writing all those silly things at the start of my letter. When I was watching the film, I felt how lucky I am to have parents like you and Maman. But when I started writing, I forgot all my happiness, and I just ended up complaining to you. Please forgive me for being ungrateful.

Mrs. Basteh-negar invited the families to their house this afternoon to be together on *Sizdah Be-dar*, and also to have a meeting. I shouldn't talk about food, but I really can't ignore the delicious *Ash reshteh*[17] we ate there. It would be great if we were allowed to send you home-cooked meals! Don't you agree?

Last year on this day, we went out for a walk in Darabad. Do you remember? We took our *Sabzeh*[18] to throw it away. I knotted some of the grass blades from the *Sabzeh* while making my wishes. You know, Baba, none of them were granted, and I blame you for that. By tradition, we should throw the *Sabzeh* into the river on thirteenth day of the New Year, but you never let me to do that. Why? *Because it would contaminate the water, disturb the ecosystem, distort the visual and physical*

---

17      ·*Ash reshteh* is a kind of thick soup that consists of different beans, vegetables, and noodles, traditionally eaten on the thirteenth day of *Nowruz*.

18      *Sabzeh* (sprouts) is one element of the *Haft Seen* that might have sprouted from wheat, lentils, barley, or mung beans.

*landscape, etc.* I know all of that! But when I threw the *Sabzeh* in the garbage instead of a river, my wishes couldn't be granted! Instead, they're just buried under piles of garbage, rather than flowing in the river.

Don't be mad at me! I threw this year's *Sabzeh* into the Darband River before going to Mr. Basteh-negar's house. Please overlook this one-off action, okay? This way, my wishes might have a chance of being granted. Do you want to know what they were? I made a wish that you and the others would get released soon, and also for Mohammad to pass the entrance exam so that he can go to university.

(God, please grant my wishes to show my father that I am right. Amen.)

I suppose you want to know what the women did in today's meeting. They decided to go to the Revolutionary Court tomorrow and ask for a visiting time. I don't think that the families of any other prisoners have gone to the Court as much as these women have. This is now part of their routine and daily actions.

The first days of your arrest were as much of an unpredictable shock for the Revolutionary Court as for the families. They had been bewildered and flustered by families' actions, and therefore tried to prevent them from continuing like this by ignoring, threatening, and insulting them. However, the families stood their ground, constantly going to the Court and demanding their rights.

The biggest concern of the families at the moment is your mental health, as you are all in solitary confinement and don't have access to any news. One of the women said a very normal psychological response in persons who are isolated for a long time is that they start to easily accept what they are told. She said in that situation, the prisoner starts believing his interrogator and thinks the news he is given might be true. Oh, Baba, this is dreadful. I don't want to even think about it.

I miss you so much, but I will be strong and tolerate being away from you. Promise me that you will be strong too, and that you can tolerate being alone in your confinement. Baba, don't believe their news, just believe what we say to you. Do you promise me?

Love you.

*Tuesday, 3 April, 2001*
*11:40 pm*

Maman and some other women went to the Revolutionary Court today, but still no updates from you – as I expected. No one is responsive about your situation. But these women never give up. They gathered again in the evening at Uncle Reza's home and decided to hold a public commemoration for *Ashura*[19] and even to invite two speakers.

The families' letter to the UN Commissioner of Human Rights was also read aloud at the meeting. It still needs some modification, but everyone agrees on its structure. It will be sent to the UN very soon.

You know, Baba, I've attended almost all the meetings with Maman. I sit silently in a corner, looking at the women and listening carefully to their discussions. Today, in the middle of the meeting, when the women were engaged with the letter to the UN, I thought to myself that I have the same role as a historian. In olden times, historians witnessed events without taking much part in them. They documented what they saw and heard – just like me, but with one little difference (or maybe big): I also add my feelings to the writings.

At school, I've read some texts from the old historians in our Farsi literature books. They wrote in a very literary style, using archaic words. Maybe I should try to write like them:

"On the fourteenth day of the splendid spring, in the year 1380 recorded in the Solar Hijri calendar, a gathering of women, whose husbands were arrested by the Revolutionary Court on the accusation of conspiring to overthrow the Islamic Republic of Iran, did discuss the means by which they could prove the

---

19      The day of Ashura is commemorated by Shi'a Muslims as a day of mourning for the martyrdom of Imam Hossein, the grandson of the Prophet Muhammad at the Battle of Karbala on 10 Muharram in the year 61 AH (680 AD).

innocence of their husbands. The gathering was held in the dwelling of one of the arrestees, Reza Raiss-Tousi, who resided in northern Tehran..."

And I perhaps should finish it like this:

"I, Maryam *Al-Saltaneh* (I gave a title to myself), known as Anna, observed and documented the meeting for posterity to serve as evidence of the efforts of Iranian women in the cause of justice and freedom in the early twenty-first century."

Shall I continue like this? I'm sorry, but I think I prefer my own approach.

This evening has been so gloomy and boring. No entertaining programs on TV. And I haven't been in the mood to do anything. You know what I just did? I read over the letters that you previously wrote to me.

I am so happy with myself now because I used to write letters to you when you were busy and I couldn't find you, or when I was angry with you. If we'd just talked, then I would have nothing to read and recall you by these days.

I'd always put my letters between the pages of the book that you were reading. It was easy to find the right book, always open, face-down upon your bedside table. Then, on the following morning, your letter to me would be on my desk in a closed envelope, always addressed with the same bold letters: Direct – Confidential. It made me feel important.

Baba, your last book is still open on your bedside table. So far, I've written seventeen letters to you.

I wish you could write me a Direct – Confidential letter every night!

Miss you.

*Friday, 6 April, 2001*
*11:20 am*

Good morning Baba,

I suppose you impatiently want to know about the *Ashura* ceremony, but can you guess what happened?

Our plans didn't go as they had been organized. On Tuesday —a day before *Ashura*—one of the women, in an interview with Radio France, mentioned our planned gathering for that day. The speakers were concerned that the ceremony had been publicized on the media and said that they wouldn't come. You know, there is always the worry of another raid or arrest at any gatherings!

We were stuck in a dilemma. It was understood that we wouldn't have a speaker, plus there was the risk of a raid by the Court agents. But many of us wanted to pray together and not give up.

In the end, the families of the arrestees decided to hold an intimate gathering at Uncle Reza's home and pray together on the night of *Ashura*. We were united as one family with the same grief and difficulties, with the same prayers and the same wishes.

We prayed for those in any kind of need or trouble, for all those suffering, for the oppressed, and for those in prison... When the prayer reached this part, everyone burst into tears and said the prayer louder.

The lights were turned off, but I could see in the dim light of the candles that some held the holy Quran on their heads, and some just kept it tightly in their hands. They would then lift their hand up and repeat the prayers from bottom of their hearts, while slightly swaying back and forth or right and left. Such unique and spiritual moments, as if God was there and listening to all of our prayers.

I prayed for you, Baba. For all of you.

What did you do? Did you pray, too? I hope you've at least had a Quran to read and soothe yourself.

These days, I am reading Maxim Gorky's novel, *Mother.* Last summer, I had read his *Childhood*, which I really loved. But

*Mother* is something special. I didn't even know that we had it on our bookshelves. Your overloaded bookshelves, Baba!!

Do you know how I found it? Here's the story:

Some days after your arrest, Maman put some books from the bookshelves into boxes to store them somewhere else, outside our house. I didn't tell you at the time, as I really feared that the Revolutionary Court agents would raid our house, read my letters, and find out about this. (I am still scared of their raids, but I found a good place to hide my letters, so I can tell you now.)

But can you guess where I am hiding the letters? You may have three guesses.

- Underneath the Carpet? Wrong.
- Inside the mattress cover? Wrong.
- Under flower pots outside the window? Wrong.

I hide them in the freezer, underneath the frozen foods! Isn't it smart?

Anyway, the books that Maman packed were old-looking, with low-quality, straw-colored papers. She said they were published only once, during the first and second years of the Revolution, and never reprinted again. She explained, "They are very rare and document the Revolution from different people's perspectives."

Apparently, we had had these treasures in our home all these years, and I never looked at them. It was a pity, because when finally I found out about them, we had to conceal our treasure again! Maman's aim was to hide these books in the event of a raid by the Revolutionary Court agents. She said they might never return back what they confiscate (which would be a kind of robbery, wouldn't it?).

Baba dear, don't worry! We've already taken care to prevent losing our treasured books. They are safe and sound.

Oh, sorry, I told you this long story to reach this point: from packing away the books, I found *Mother,* which was hidden somewhere behind other books. Maman said it was among the forbidden books before the Revolution. Why does every system have its forbidden books? Politics is *very* confusing for me!

While I am reading *Mother,* I unconsciously compare our Revolution, you, Maman, and even myself to the Revolutionary actions of the factory workers in the book, Pavel, and his mother. The story felt very familiar to me, as if I had lived it myself. Is that strange? Or did you have the same feeling when you first read it?

It seems that standing up against oppression and following the truth has the same consequences all over the world. In one part of the book, Pavel tells his mother, "We are not doing anything wrong, but we can expect to be imprisoned." This brought tears to my eyes and reminded me of you.

Why should you be in prison, Baba? Why? Why? *Why?*

I meant to write a short letter, just to tell you what happened on *Ashura,* but once I get started, I seem to have an active pen. I am going to stop it here.

Love you.

*Saturday, 7 April, 2001*
*10:15 pm*

Dear Baba Hossein,

Today was the first day of school after a loooooooooooong holiday, but we've forgotten that we ever had a vacation. We had Farsi literature exam today and other examinations will come one after another!!

Not many at school know about you. Just my very close friends. I don't want to tell anyone. It doesn't mean that I am ashamed, embarrassed, a coward, or anything else. You do know that I am proud of you. However, since your arrest, everything has changed at home. We don't have our previous normal life. We face shocking news on TV, from newspapers, and at the Court all the time. We also receive many visitors and phone calls every day from people who constantly ask about you and want to know the news. So, we need to repeat all the bad and stressful news over and over.

The home environment is very tense and stressful, but I'll try to keep my school life the same as before, as much as I can; it is the only place where I can be away from this hustle and bustle. I just want to have my usual conversations and relationships with the girls at school. I don't want everybody ask me about you every day and give me strange or pitiful looks due to news and media broadcasts.

Many girls at our school don't have any clue about politics, let alone know what a political prisoner is! The important things for them are their appearance and boys. So, Baba, do you understand now why I don't want to tell anyone at school about you? But if they find out and ask me, I will proudly talk about you. It would be my pleasure.

This morning, Maman went to the University of Tehran to talk with your colleagues. She said they are very upset about your condition and they will definitely support you. Some of your students also came to her and asked about you.

Baba, you should be at the university, not in prison!

I always keep all the bad news for the end. I want to escape far away from it, but there is no way out from reality. Are you ready to hear?

Many members of *Nehzat-e Azadi*[20] were arrested today in a sudden attack on them in their homes, in the streets, and in their offices. It was a massive arrest and not a good sign at all! Nobody knows what is going on.

May God bless you and keep you safe.

P.S. I tried to study for my geology lesson but I couldn't concentrate. Please pray for me so our teacher won't give an exam for it tomorrow.

---

20    *Nehzat-e Azadi* is an Iranian pro-democracy political party founded in 1961.

*Sunday, 8 April, 2001*
*Midnight*


Hello Baba,

Yesterday's arrests have led to great concern. Many people called and dropped in these two days to ask about you. We still have some visitors who are talking with Maman in the living room. However, our knowledge is the same as others'. We haven't had any phone calls from you for *two weeks* and the Revolutionary Court just keeps saying that "everything is under investigation and they will reveal the subversive documents very soon!"

Maman says that if they had any documents, they would have publicized them by now! So, if there are no documents, why won't they release you? Many say that they are forcing you to give a false confession to be broadcasted on TV! Is that true? I hope not.

Baba, can you believe I fell asleep in biology class today? I know, I should sleep earlier at nights, but I can't. We have visitors 'til late and I can't sleep when I hear their voices. I don't know how Mohammad handles it! He tells me I am too curious and want to find out all kinds of things. "You don't want to miss any conversation," he just told me few minutes ago, when I was nagging about this situation.

Mmmm, maybe he is right. But it's not bad, is it? Otherwise, I can't tell you everything.

There should be a better solution for this! What if the people don't come here after 9:00 in the evening and give us some privacy? What do you think?

Don't be mad at me! I am not disrespectful to the people who are worried about you and call us and/or come here because of you, and also, of course, us. On the contrary, I am very thankful for their support and care, which is priceless and helps us to stay strong. *But*, it's a very critical time of year for Mohammad and I. My final exams will start in two months and he has an entrance exam for university in July. We both need to concentrate on our studies and it's *impossible*.

Do you think now that I am an ungrateful, rude, and thankless girl? But, Baba, you don't have any idea about the atmosphere of our home after your arrest, so you don't have the right to scold me. Sorry for being too frank!

It seems that our visitors are leaving. I will go to say goodbye and then sleep right away.

Good night.

*Monday, 9 April, 2001*
*Midnight*


Dear Baba Hossein,
*Happy birthday!*
Dr. Maleki's family was here tonight. We dined together and afterwards, we celebrated both his son, Abouzar's, and your birthday. We sang a birthday song and then Abouzar blew out the candles on behalf of you and himself and we all wished for Dr. Maleki's and your freedom.

Baba, those who detain you are so mean and merciless. Don't they have a family themselves? Don't they understand how much we've missed you? They even didn't let you call us on your birthday! How can I say happy birthday to you?

Maman and Mrs. Maleki then did the final edits of the letter to Mary Robinson, who is the UN Commissioner of Human Rights. The letter is about the violation of human rights in your case; the raiding of a private residence and confiscating your things, keeping you in solitary confinement in an undisclosed detention center, using psychological pressure to extract a confession, not having access to lawyers, threatening the families to be silent about you, and many other things. It's a comprehensive letter describing the condition of all of you in detail. It will be sent tomorrow and will hopefully be helpful in changing your situation.

You know, before your arrest, I didn't know anything about human rights. Kind of a shame for someone who wants to be a UN Secretary General, isn't it?

I heard about it for the first time from Narges, Mr. Rahmani's[21] wife. On that day, outside the Court, she was talking with other women and I heard "human rights" among her words, which made me kind of curious. Literally, I understood the meaning of the term, but I wanted to know what kind of rights she was talking about, exactly.

---

21      A member of the *Melli-Mazhabi* Coalition.

Through the women's meetings, I've learned many things, and one of the most interesting has been human rights. Now, I know about the Universal Declaration of Human Rights, and this makes me feel more confident because from now on, I'm aware of all my rights and I could defend them anywhere in the world.

Did you know that Iran voted for this declaration? It's ironic, isn't it? They don't respect it at all. By detaining you, they violate our rights every day, every hour, and every minute...

Baba, I miss you. Please come back home.

*Tuesday, 10 April, 2001*
*11:30 pm*

*One month* has passed! Can you believe it?

We've never been away from each other for this long. That night, I thought you would be released very soon. I didn't imagine that it would become this serious and complicated. It was exciting for me at first, but it is not any more. I want you to come back home. I haven't seen you for a month and I haven't talked to you for *sixteen days*!! What are you doing there?

Is it stupid that I've been writing a letter to you every day since your arrest, while I know you won't read it, and I cannot send it to you? But I really do love to write to you. It relieves all the pain. When I am writing to you, I forget that you are in prison and I forget we haven't heard from you for a long time. In those moments, I immerse myself in my writing and feel that you are right here, with me, listening to me. Would you like me to tell you something?

I've never felt so close to you as I do now. I don't hide anything from you in my letters. I write impulsively and freely about everything and if you have a chance to read them one day, you might think, "this is not my daughter!" But this is me; my true self.

By the way, Dr. Peyman had a family visit at the Revolutionary Court today. That was his second visiting time since you were arrested. I wish we could have one, too! But it's good; at least we could get some information about one of you. He told his wife, "Go and visit any authority you can; the Supreme Leader, the president and..." It seems that he must be under a tremendous amount of pressure to have said such a thing.

I miss you, Baba.

*Friday, 13 April, 2001*
*11:15 am*

Hello Baba,

Last night, I was so overwhelmed with different feelings – anger, anxiety, and worry – that I didn't write to you. I cannot put into words how I've felt.

It was around 4:00 in the evening that someone called home. He told me in a very kind tone, "I'm your mother's friend. Give the phone to her." I recognized his voice; he was Seyed Majid. Although I've seen him just once, even now his voice is imprinted in my mind and I don't think I could ever erase it.

He told Maman that she could talk to you. I pressed the speaker button to hear your voice.

You were not fine at all. It seemed you were sleepy or disoriented!

Maman asked you whether you need a lawyer and you said, "I don't know."

"Can I have a lawyer?" you asked someone there.

Apparently, there were some people who listened to your conversation as well as Seyed Majid. We could hear their voices, but from a far distance.

Someone told you, "you could, but if any information from your file leaks outside, it would be your own fault." He was threatening you!

This is ridiculous. What kind of confidential information is in your file for them to threaten you like this?!

You told Maman, "Okay. Take a lawyer." I really admired your courage at that moment. You didn't give in to their threat.

You asked about Maman's heart and told her not to put too much pressure on herself. Then you asked that guy, "Can I tell my wife to sell the car if she needs money?" and he replied, "No, tell her when you meet her."

But Maman didn't wait for your reaction and told you, "Don't worry. Everything is fine here."

I was so furious. You were engaged in a normal family conversation and yet you needed someone else's permission to discuss every single matter!

Maman said, "Anna wants to talk to you."

Again you asked him, "Can I talk to my children?"

He said, "Okay."

Really! I should thank them for their kindness to let me talk to my father after *eighteen* days!!

I took the phone while my heart was beating so fast that I could hear its beat in my ears. But I took a deep breath, swallowed my saliva, and then, with a cheerful voice, I told you, "Happy birthday, Baba dear."

You said, "Thank you, but when was my birthday?"

I instantly froze. You didn't remember your own birthday?! OMG, you didn't remember your birthday! What did they do to you? All the stories about psychological torture and giving drugs to prisoners to confuse them passed through my mind in those two seconds. I looked at Maman and she encouraged me with her glance to talk to you.

"April ninth," I told you.

Then you said, "Ah, okay. When I come back, we'll buy a cake and celebrate together."

Baba, I know you weren't good at all. You were not in a normal condition. I felt it.

You told me to pursue my classes and study my lessons. Mohammad wasn't at home, so you said I should tell him to study for his exam and not pay attention to anything.

In a second, I thought I should just give you some kind of encouraging news, even if they will hang up the phone. So I told you, "Your friends, your colleagues and your students say hi to you and support you."

"Say hello to everyone," you said. And then we said goodbye.

We talked longer this time, but you weren't fine at all.

I was so angry, upset, and anxious. I asked Maman, "Did you hear that Baba didn't remember his birthday?" She tried to calm me down by saying that you're always busy and never remember anybody's birthday, let alone your own. But I know that she is also very worried about you.

Baba, maybe they are brainwashing you? I can't even think about it. My God, please, please, please keep my father safe.

We had a lot of good news for you, but we were concerned about telling you on the phone. They've forbidden us to talk about issues that aren't related to the family and we're afraid they will stop these few phone calls if we tell you other news. It's really unfair! It is so humiliating and so oppressive!!

Baba, please be strong. Many people are supporting you. I tried to tell you that in my last sentence. Hopefully you sensed what I meant!

Yesterday morning, Maman met the Deputy Minister of Science at the Ministry of Science. He told her that three ministers (of Science, Health, and Intelligence) are supposed to write a report for President Khatami, regarding you and the other arrestees. He said that the government is following the case very carefully and willing to solve it.

Baba, I miss you so much. I thought if you called I would feel better, but since yesterday, I've felt terribly awful. I am worried about you. Dreadful thoughts come to my mind. Are they torturing you?

Please be strong.

*Saturday, 14 April, 2001*
*11:20 pm*

Dear Baba,

You can't imagine how happy I am now. Are you going to say that I don't have a mental balance? One day happy, one day sad, and one day neutral! But this is it. My feelings change depending on your situation and the news, and I can't do anything about it.

So, do you want to know what's happened?

I was ready to go to bed when you called. You sounded fresh and energetic, totally different than on Thursday. It was a very big surprise that you called after only two days; however, I think this was due to Maman's arguing at the Court.

This morning, she went to the Revolutionary Court to bring the stuff you had asked for on Thursday; some shampoo, a towel, and underwear. I wonder how you've taken a shower until now if none of these things are available there! I also sent you a bar of chocolate as your birthday gift and two books (they didn't accept the books).

At the Court, Maman complained about your previous call and said you seemed very distracted. She got angry and blamed them for your psychological situation, but Seyed Majid insisted that you are fine and to prove this, he would let you call again tonight. And you did.

It was a short call. You just talked with Maman and told her that you've received the stuff and even the chocolate! This time, you firmly told Maman to hire a lawyer and ask him to go to the Court and read your file as soon as possible.

I don't know if you were pretending or if you were really fine! Maybe they made you talk to us like this?! Nevertheless, I felt that you are much better than the previous time, and now I am the happiest girl in the world.

Good night from your happy daughter.

*Sunday, 15 April, 2001*
*10:00 pm*

Hello Baba,

This isn't a real letter; it's just a short note to say that I am a very busy student this week and I'm going to write a letter pretty soon when exams are over.

Tomorrow, I have a geology exam; the day after tomorrow, I have a chemistry exam; and the day after that, I have biology exam. I hate exams!!

But, I love you.

P.S. I forgot to tell you that the Islamic Association of Students and the science faculty of the University of Tehran just issued a statement today regarding you. They expressed their concern about your arrest and they mentioned that continuing to detain you without providing any evidence for the accusations is unfair.

I told you that many people are supporting you. Just be strong.

*Monday, 16 April, 2001*
*Midnight*


Dear Baba Hossein,

It's impossible to be calm for even one day!! I knew that my happiness wouldn't last for a long time! They are playing with us! They are very bad guys. Don't trust them at all!

I don't know how to tell you the bad news? I hate to write bad news!

The Revolutionary Court agents raided the magazine's office today. They searched everywhere from 11:00-5:00 and confiscated everything; the computers' hard drives, the archives, the interview tapes, the floppies, your writings… everything, Baba, *everything*.

Maman and the other employees were working hard to publish the new issue of *Chemistry & Development* for next week, but it is impossible now. All their efforts have become fruitless! Nothing is left. They took everything with them.

After publishing five issues, and when the magazine has established its place and started flourishing, we have to stop it. Why? I really don't know the answer!

The agents didn't let the employees call Maman, so we only found out when they had left the office. Maman and I went to the office right away. Everyone looked anxious and tired.

I looked all over; papers were strewn around, the desk and cabinet drawers were wide open and emptied. The wastepaper bins were emptied on the floor. Can you believe they even took the crumpled wastepaper from the bins? They *plowed up* the office. I couldn't find any description better than this!

I don't understand what they were looking for in a scientific magazine's office? Perhaps they really believe their own lie that you are a subversive and this office is the place for making bombs?!

Baba, today, for the first time in my life, I felt profoundly desperate and miserable. They have all the power, but what do we have? Nothing. Maman says we have God. But why does God allow them to oppress us? *Why?*

Only we know how much energy and effort you put into this magazine. Every evening, weekend, and holiday over the past two years, you would be working hard in this office to make your dreams come true. Through this magazine, you wanted to reform the teaching of chemistry in the education system and make it more practical, provide new strategies for producing chemical products, improve the chemical industry, and many other good things, which I've been unable to understand. You wanted all of these for your country, and now you are accused of being subversive!! This is ridiculous!

I'm sorry, I cannot continue writing any more, Baba dear. I feel very bad. I feel a pressure in my head and my throat aches, as if something is stuck in it.

Miss you, and need your hug more than ever.

P.S. It's 2:00 am and I couldn't sleep. I was looking over the previous issues of *Chemistry & Development* magazine. You know what grabbed my attention? The quote from Linus Pauling just above the content page: "Every aspect of the world today – even politics and international relations – is affected by chemistry."

You told me this quote once, when I asked you how someone could be a chemist and also a political activist. To be honest, I still can't understand the relationship between chemistry and politics, but if you and Pauling say so, then there must be something there!! And maybe I will find it out one day!

*Tuesday, 17 April, 2001*
*10:30 pm*

Dear Baba,

I only slept for four hours last night. I was thinking the whole night about what they would do to our home if they raided it! Can you imagine what would happen if they emptied the bookshelves in my room? It's my nightmare now.

I was also thinking about these agents and their job; to raid and search people's dwellings! I read in Gorki's book, when Pavel's house is raided, one of his friends says, "These agents have the dirtiest job in the world, and they themselves know it!"

Do you think they know their job is really bad? I don't think so. If they knew, they would never do this.

What about those people who eavesdrop on our phone conversations without our permission? Since your arrest, I feel that our phone is being tapped. When I pick up the phone, I hear a voice, as if someone else is connected to the conversation. During the phone calls, the quality of the sound drops and my voice echoes. And at the end of the calls, I hear a voice again, that perhaps represents the disconnection of the third party from the line. Do you think I am hallucinating? But this is what I feel nowadays!

I can't talk with my friends comfortably anymore, because I don't want them to listen to my private conversations. I think eavesdropping is also among the dirtiest jobs in the world. Don't you agree with me?

I'm too sleepy, Baba. Recently, I am making this an excuse, am I not? But everything is disrupted these days. Apart from all these happenings, school also makes me really tired.

I wish that you'd come back home and everything would be the same as before.

Good night.

*Wednesday, 18 April, 2001*
*Midnight*

Hello Baba,

This is very disappointing, but I'll tell you: I really messed up all my exams this week. I got 15.25/20 for geology, 13.5/20 for chemistry, and 14.5/20 for biology.

Are you shocked? I find it kind of weird myself to have these marks! During the last eleven years in school, I've never had a mark under 18/20, and suddenly facing these low marks is kind of shocking! But you know, I am not that upset because I really couldn't study and this is all out of my control.

My teachers were all surprised with my marks; however, I think my biology teacher knows about you. When she was announcing the marks in class, she said, "I know those who got 14/20 have had a problem, otherwise they could get a better mark." She indirectly hinted at me, I guess.

Baba, I want you to come back home. Could you please do me a favor and come back home?

I know, I am the meanest daughter in the world right now. I know you are not in prison by choice, and still I started insisting you come back! I am just a very stupid girl who makes you feel upset.

Please forgive me.

*Sunday, 22 April, 2001*
*11:00 pm*

Dear Baba,

Today was Sunday, and like every Sunday, I was nervous for no reason. This feeling has made me hate Sundays lately! But I just found out that there is a reason behind my hatred; the day you were arrested was a Sunday. Do you remember that dark Sunday? *Forty-two* days have passed since then!

In the days after it was raided, Maman has been busy with the magazine office, organizing and cleaning the mess the agents had left behind. She wrote a statement to the press about the raid and explained what happened on that day. She mentioned in the statement that the Revolutionary Court had confiscated everything and it's now impossible to print the new issue of *Chemistry & Development* magazine.

I am still very upset about the raid. To be honest, I don't want to believe that it actually happened. I feel it was just a nightmare and I will open my eyes one day and won't remember it.

The telephone rang just a minute ago and I thought it might be you. I ran to the phone, but it wasn't you. It has been a week and you haven't called us. You've probably heard about the raid of the magazine office. Don't think about it, Baba. Everything's gonna be okay. You will publish it again when you are released, won't you?

I miss you more than you can imagine. I think about you all the time and I know you do the same.

Be strong, my dear Baba.

*Wednesday, 25 April, 2001*
*6:30 am*

Hello Baba Hossein,

My school bus will come in a few minutes, but I couldn't go without writing to you and telling you how much I miss you these days, although I write less often than before.

You might think that I've gotten used to your absence? Wrong. I never, never, never get used to your absence. I am just a bit busy with my studies at school.

Good news: *one hundred and nine* university professors around the country signed the appeal letter to President Khatami and sent it to him. They stand in support of you and defend your right to freedom of expression.

Many say this is a historical letter. This is the first time that such a number of scholars have demanded something from a president in the history of the Islamic Republic of Iran. The news of the letter was not only covered by newspapers in Iran, but also, as we have seen, it has been reported by foreign media.

Day by day, more voices rise up to defend your rights, and this is so priceless, isn't it? I wish you could see the letter and knew how your colleagues are supporting you.

I am impatiently waiting for Mr. Khatami's reaction. Until now, he has not directly or publicly reacted to your case, but maybe this time he will and will answer this letter. What do you think?

*Oh, oh,* Baba, I should go. Mr. Chizari, my bus driver, is honking his one-minute warning.

I'll write to you later.

*Thursday, 26 April, 2001*
*Midnight*

Have I told you before that you've been in the headlines of the politics pages of newspapers since your arrest? There is always something about you, whether in your favor or against it.

Sometimes, even on the same page, the views of your opponents and supporters are published together; the comments of the head of the Revolutionary Court (which is against you) is written next to the views of MPs and the Intelligence Minister, who speak in support of you. I think despite the crackdowns and the closures of many newspapers during last year, we still have a kind of freedom of the press in this country, don't you agree?

Today, while I was archiving the essays and news that I had cut out of newspapers, I thought that if you had been arrested in the 80s or 90s, then no newspaper could publish content like this. Or, even before the Revolution, there hadn't been freedom of the press like today. Who dared to write or talk about political prisoners? The Reformist newspapers have broken the biased nature of the press.

I clearly recall the day you took me to one of your meetings. A guest speaker talked about the advent of the first Reformist newspaper. It was just a few months after the seventh presidential election; everyone was joyful about Mr. Khatami's victory and eagerly waiting for new changes in the country. Can you believe four years have passed since then?!

The speaker grabbed my attention with his passionate speech. Actually, it was not just me; everyone in that meeting was completely spellbound. He heralded big changes in the Iranian press, a kind of revolution. His voice is still inside my head: "We plan to publish the country's most widely-read newspaper, and our goal is to print it three times a day with updates." I later found out he was Mr. Shamsolvaezin, Editor-in-Chief of the *Jame'eh* newspaper.[22]

---

22      *Jame'eh* is the first Reformist independent newspaper (February 1998 – July 1998).

He was right. The *Jameh'eh* newspaper started publishing a few months later, and during its short lifetime – before being shut down by the Conservatives – it had achieved the goals which Mr. Shamsolvaezin had set in that meeting. It has also become the standard for other Reformist newspapers which were born afterwards, hasn't it?

The Reformist newspapers are so helpful for delivering our voices to the authorities and society. As much as the Conservatives' media tries to condemn you and represent you as criminals, the Reformist newspapers try to reveal the truth. Their pressure on the Revolutionary Court, Parliament, and government is undeniable. When you read my archive, you'll see for yourself.

You know, Baba, I really feel lucky to live in this era and experience some freedom, no matter how little and short-lived. I hope the newspapers can resist the Conservatives' oppression. Do you think they could, or will this freedom become restricted gradually?

The sound of rain dropping on the ivy leaves in the garden creates a soothing symphony. I'm going to sleep with this symphony and think about you.

Good night.

*Friday, 27 April, 2001*
*10:30 pm*


Hello Baba,

Can you guess where I was today? Sangan Fall.

Mr. and Mrs. Arab[23] kindly invited me to go there with them. There were also about twenty other people from their extended family. I was the only non-family member among them, but they all warmly welcomed me and sympathized with your situation. You know, people sometimes pamper me because of your imprisonment. And to be honest, I like it!!

The weather was wonderful, sunny with a mild spring breeze. All of the hillside along our way to the waterfall was covered by rhubarb plants. And all along the way, I was busy picking and eating rhubarbs. They were so tasty, fresh, sour, and watery. Please don't say I'm a gourmand! If you were me, you would do the same.

Baba, do you remember last summer, when we went to Sangan Fall together?

Today, I recalled all the moments of that day. After three hours of hiking to reach the fall, the only thing I wanted so badly on that hot day was to stand under the waterfall. It was the first time for me being so close to a waterfall; I was excited and amazed.

Many people were around; the boys and men were playing under the waterfall, but the girls and women sat on the rocks, watching the fall or just dipping their feet in the water's edge. That was one of the times that I had preferred to be a boy!

But you playfully pushed me into the water and encouraged me to go under the waterfall. With your encouragement, I finally waded into the water. It was cold. The spray stung my face and I couldn't hear anything over the sound of the waterfall. I was completely soaked in just two seconds. It was the most joyful experience that I've had!!

But, today, I couldn't go under the waterfall. I missed you so

---

23      Family friends.

badly. I sat on a rock and looked at the others playing there. I saw a father who grabbed his daughters' hands and took them under the fall. He reminded me of you. I was jealous of them at that moment. I wanted you there.

Baba, in my heart I thank you, always, for the life, freedom, and independence that you and Maman have given me. I know that many girls in this country crave these things. I thank you also for all your encouragement and support in helping me to follow my dreams. You've always told me, "Don't let the restrictions on women in this country hinder your dreams." And you've always tried to give me the same opportunities as Mohammad, despite the inequalities that exist in our country. Every day, more than ever, I realize how special you've been and how I really miss you!

I didn't tell you how proud I felt to be your daughter and how much your support meant to me that summer's day, when we went to Sangan Waterfall together. Is it too late to tell you now?

I miss being able to hug you, kiss you, and feel you. I still need to learn many things from you. I still need your support. I need you, Baba dear.

Please come back home.

*Saturday, 28 April, 2001*
*10:00 pm*

Here is some news. Bad news!

The Revolutionary Court broadcasted a new statement on TV today. I recorded it for you. They repeated again that you are members of a subversive group and that they've brought up new charges against you: "contact with The Mojahedin Khalq Organization,[24]" "insulting religious values," and "applying armed tactics"!!

None of their accusations are acceptable, but *armed tactics*?! Seriously? Who believes this one? Where is the evidence for it? They can't just accuse you without having any evidence!

Each of these charges could have a death sentence! OMG, how can I write this?!

I thought I'd gotten used to this kind of news, but I was wrong. Every time I hear new statements, I get shocked again and my heart pounds so loudly in my ears, it feels as if I am going to become deaf. I want to go in my room, shut the door, put my hands over my ears, and stay alone, without hearing any voices. But I never do this. I just stay around and pretend that nothing important has happened. I don't want to make Maman and Mohammad even more upset.

You know, Baba, all of us try to act like this. Maman, Mohammad, and I are trying to be strong for each other. But I can see in Maman's and Mohammad's eyes that they feel just like I do.

After this statement was broadcasted, many people called to ask about you. But we haven't heard from you for *two weeks*! How can we tell people about you when we don't have any news ourselves?!

Now, I'm a hundred percent sure that they are forcing you to make a false confession on TV and confirm their bullshit!

---

24     The Mojahedin Khalq Organization (MKO) is a hardline militant cult operating outside Iran and is intent on overthrowing Iranian government to take control of the State.

Because of that, they keep you far from any contact with others. They won't let us visit or even talk to you regularly. They don't want you to know that people have never believed their lies. They don't want you to know that so many people are supporting you outside the prison.

Baba, please be strong and don't believe them. Promise me that you will resist all of their pressure, okay?

I'll write to you later. Love you, Baba dear.

*Sunday, 29 April, 2001*
*9:30 pm*

Hello Baba Hossein,

The routine and mundane life continues at school. I haven't mentioned any lessons and exams recently, but we are still having them every day. I'm doing my best to concentrate on my studies, but believe me, it's impossible with all these happenings.

Maman and the wives of the other arrestees went to Parliament today. After yesterday's statement, they are even more determined to prove that you're innocent and make efforts for you to be released.

They talked to many parliamentary representatives. The Article 90[25] Commission assured the women that their complaint against the Judiciary is being followed with great care. And the Medical Commission told them that they are very concerned about your health and detention conditions, and very soon they will send a committee to survey the prisons. The Health Minister, Dr. Farhadi, was coincidentally at Parliament, and he has also promised to collaborate with them. However, I doubt they could find you in any prison! No one knows where you are detained!

You see, Baba, the government and Parliament are with you. They care about you. They've stood in front of the Revolutionary Court's charges filed against you and constantly said, "There are no documents or any evidence to show that you are subversive." The whole situation seems to be a power struggle between two parties: Reformists and Conservatives. However, it is you and your comrades who are being so oppressively sacrificed in their battle. But why you?

This is a question that has beset me for some time, now. The only answer that comes to mind is that they're afraid of

---

25    Article 90 of Iran's Constitution puts Parliament in charge of investigating complaints made about the operation of the Parliament, the Executive, and the Judiciary. A commission – appointed by Iran's Parliament – governs this process and is called the Article 90 Commission.

your popularity among the university students, as well as other strata in society. I think they are particularly alarmed by last year's parliamentary elections, when three of the *Melli-mazhabi's* candidates won.

You had neither money nor the media support of the Reformists and Conservatives in that election, but people still voted for your candidates. I remember the only way that the *Melli-Mazhabi* Coalition campaigned was through giving speeches at the universities. If you had had more channels for outreach, you might have won more chairs in Parliament. Who knows?

Only now do I understand why the votes of your three elected candidates were unlawfully declared invalid and your representatives weren't allowed to enter Parliament: because they don't want you. They don't want the *Melli-Mazhabi's* rationale in the ruling system. Am I right?

I wish you were here and we could discuss this more. You always have answers for my questions, but now, without you, my mind has filled up with tons of questions, to which I can barely find any answers. I miss you and miss our discussions!

P.S. Just now, I dissected a sheep's brain in the kitchen. So cool! It was practice for my biology lab exam tomorrow. Wish me good luck!

# MAY

*Tuesday, 1 May, 2001*
*Midnight*

Dear Baba Hossein,
I was exclusively occupied with studying for my biology exam when you called yesterday evening. Same as always, it was a short and monitored conversation.

I asked you if you've lost weight, and your answer was obviously a *yes*. I don't know why on Earth I asked you this question! I'm always very flustered and I never know what to say!

Every time you call, I first get excited and joyful from hearing your voice, but then anxiety and anger replace my joy. The anxiety that I start to feel while I am talking to you and in the days that follow is indescribable. I review our short conversations in my mind over and over 'til I get a headache. I blame myself: "why did I say this!" or "why didn't I say that!"

Yesterday, you told me, "Don't be upset. These problems are common in third world countries. We should be patient on the way to democracy. Sooner or later, all the problems will be solved." But do you really believe in what you said?

Baba, nothing is okay here or where you are. They are torturing you, but they also torture those of us at home. Mohammad and I can't concentrate on our studies. Maman has stopped all her social life and dedicated her time to advocate for you. They have not only imprisoned you, they have imprisoned us all. This is a collective punishment!!

You've been in prison for *fifty days* without access to your lawyer. You are accused of heavy charges without any evidence. You are not allowed to visit your family and our few conversations are monitored. Is it okay? No, it's not okay and it's not fair at all.

I hate them. I hate all those who arrested you, who interrogate you, and particularly, I hate those who dial our phone number, stand there, and watch you talking to us. I can't bear to think that they humiliate you after our phone calls by hinting at your emotions about us. In my imagination, when we say goodbye and you hang up, one of them takes the phone from you and, with a sneer on his face, says, "You miss your children? Huh?" Or, with a fake compassionate voice, he tells you, "Do you want to meet your family? If you collaborate with us, maybe I could do something for you," and so on. These imagined scenarios bombard my mind after each of our phone calls—they hurt me to the core.

Baba, I miss you a lot, but if they bother you after our phone calls, please don't call us again. I want you to stay strong in front of them without showing weakness. Don't let them emotionally manipulate you. Don't let them humiliate you more than they've done. Promise me!

After your call, I became totally distracted and couldn't study any more. I woke up this morning at 4:00 to review my exam, but I was too sleepy to study. However, the exam went fine, with some help from Yasi.[26] She gave me the answers that I didn't know. It was not cheating, was it? I don't think so. Hahahaha…

Oh, I totally forgot to tell you about my very exciting news. Guess what?

Maman decided to get a stall for *Chemistry & Development* magazine in the Tehran International Book and Press Fair. Tomorrow she'll go to submit an application for that.

They raided our magazine office and prevented its future publication to silence your voice, but we won't let them achieve

---

26      My close friend and classmate.

what they want. We'll display your magazine at the fair and tell the people that you are imprisoned because of your ideals. We'll be your voice!

I can't keep open my eyes any more.

Good night.

*Friday, 4 May, 2001*
*11:00 am*

Good morning Baba,

I am sorry that I haven't written you for days. You don't mind, do you, if I am not very consistent? I've had very busy days, but believe me that wherever I go and whatever I do, you are in my mind and in my heart.

I have many things to tell you. Let me start with good news:

First, we will have a stall in the book fair, Hooraaaaaaaaaaaaaaay!! Isn't it awesome? Maman's persistent pursuits these last few days finally worked out.

Second, you'll be delighted to hear this one! On the first of May, twenty-three faculty members of the Chemistry Department of the University of Tehran sent an appeal letter to Mr. Shahroudi, Head of the Judiciary, demanding your release. They said in their letter that they know you very well and the charges against you are unfair. You see how your colleagues are defending you? I wish I could tell you about all this news, but how?

And now, do you want to hear about my graduation ceremony from high school? Of course you do.

On Wednesday evening, we had our graduation ceremony at the school hall with the attendance of mothers and teachers. I know, it's weird to have the graduation ceremony before the final exams! But this was the school principal's decision to hold it earlier this year. And you know what? Actually no one cared about that. We just wanted to have a ceremony and some fun.

We wore graduation gowns and caps, holding our symbolic diplomas, and took lots of photos. If we have a visiting time, I will bring them for you.

As part of the ceremony, our principal chose some mothers, by taking a draw, to talk about their daughters, and guess what? Maman was among them. She went up to the stage and said to the crowd, "Eleven years ago, someone asked Anna on the phone to write a note for her father, but she was only six and hadn't gone to school yet. She told that person, with a genuine honesty, 'I cannot write. I am illiterate.' This incident caused her to feel disappointed in herself, and she blamed her father and myself for not having sent her to school so that she could learn to write. When the time came and she could write her own name, her father told her, 'You are not illiterate anymore,' and I quite remember the satisfied look she gave her father with a smile of delight."

Then, Maman turned her face to me, stared in my eyes, and continued, "Today, I am telling you, my darling: you are going to get your diploma very soon and you are not illiterate at all. But there is a long journey ahead of you. The more you learn, the more you realize how little you know. Never let anyone stop you from learning and understanding." My tears were rolling down my cheeks uncontrollably while Maman was saying all this on stage.

The whole hall burst into a volley of applause after Maman's speech. She came to me and hugged me tightly. We cried in each other's arms. I don't know if it was from joy or sadness! Perhaps a mixture of both.

Baba, I missed you a lot that day.

And finally, I reach the unpleasant part, which I really don't want to write about, but I promised to tell you everything, so I will write.

I had a nightmare last night. There was a huge crowd in Uncle Reza's house. I mean, his previous house in Saadat Abad, where they lived before Aunt Farideh's death. I couldn't recognize any of the faces, but I felt that they were friends. Someone insisted that we should go to the backyard. When we stepped in the yard, I saw you and Uncle Reza standing at the end of the yard. I ran to you and everyone started applauding. You had handcuffs and shackles on your feet that hindered your movement. I hugged Uncle Reza tightly, but you didn't let me to touch you. Several times, I tried to embrace you, but you pushed me away. I thought in my dream that perhaps you had been tortured and your body was wounded or ached, and that's why you didn't let me hug you. Then, together, you stared into my eyes and told me,

"Here there is lots of corruption." In both of your eyes, I saw pain and sorrow. I burst into tears and you did, too.

I woke up in the middle of night as I was weeping into my pillow. My heart was beating so fast, and I could hardly breathe. I've tried to push away bad thoughts, but I couldn't forget your eyes. Whenever I close my eyes, your exhausted face and your tied hands and feet appear clearly in my mind and your voice rings in my ears. I never ever want to see you in that condition again.

Baba, I wish that this whole situation was just a nightmare and that tomorrow I would wake up and see you at home again! Please don't tell Maman about my nightmare. I don't want to worry her.

Miss you more than you can imagine.

P.S. Firsthand news: despite all the rumors, Mr. Khatami officially announced his candidacy for his second term of presidency this evening. Cousin Ali was at the Interior Ministry to cover the news for Reuters, and he said there were lots of national and international reporters in the room while the president was giving his emotional speech after his announcement. I can't wait to vote for him!

*Saturday, 5 May, 2001*
*10:30 pm*

Hello Baba,

Have you read *Man's Search for Meaning*? It's kind of a memoir of a survivor, Viktor Frankl, of the Auschwitz concentration camp. Mr. Ashkiani[27] gave it to me last week. I guess he wanted to tell me indirectly that your situation is not that terribly bad and there have been many people in the world who have experienced more oppressive and cruel situations than you have.

I started reading the book on Thursday and I couldn't put it down 'til I finished it. It was unbelievable what happened in Auschwitz! I had heard before about the crematorium, but I think the other things I read in the book are as dreadful as that. The people taken to the crematorium were killed once inside, but those who were not taken there were facing death on any given day and at any moment. How could a human do these things to another human?

But, you know, despite all the dark and dreadful happenings, I think the book in general gives hope to people (at least it gives me hope). Fight to stay alive in that condition instead of committing suicide, and enjoy the little happiness which the writer mentions in the book, where he shows that even in Auschwitz, everything hadn't been absolute black; people had faith to live.

"No oppression will last forever," Maman always says, and if I had doubt before, by reading this book, I believe in it now. I'm sure one day you'll be free.

Tomorrow, Maman will go to hold the stall at the book fair. It's a pity that I cannot skip my school day and go with her!

We went to the magazine office yesterday and took lots of magazines to display in the stall. The office was deserted without you. Dust covered everything, as if it has been closed for years. I checked the post box and there were piles of letters requesting subscription to the magazine. What should we answer to their requests?!

---

27     My father's friend.

Baba, I shall tell you something, but please don't worry about it. Maman recently feels a chronic pain in her left hip. She can't walk or sit comfortably. We still don't know what it is, but hopefully it won't be serious. We're waiting for the doctor's comments.

You've no idea how much I want to hug you and kiss you for just a second! I know I should be strong, but it's hard!

Love you, Baba dear.

*Tuesday, 8 May, 2001*
*8:30 pm*

Dear Baba Hossein,

I have a very, very, very big surprise for you. Until you guess what it could be, I will tell you some news.

This morning, Maman and some of the other women went to Laleh Hotel to meet Mrs. Elahe Sharifpour-Hicks, from Human Rights Watch, to talk about your condition in prison. They also met other Americans who had come to Iran to participate in the Human Rights and Dialogue Among Civilizations Conference. Maman said they were so friendly and respectfully listened to them.

After the meeting, Maman went to the book fair, as today was the opening of the fair. During the last few days, she has been super busy with preparing our stall, despite her pain. Many friends have also helped her. I couldn't give you any comments about our stall, as I haven't seen it yet. I think the soonest possible time I could be there will be the weekend. It's the end of the academic year and I cannot skip any classes, unfortunately.

Baba, have you made your guess?

Four days from now would complete two months of our not having seen each other, *but tomorrow we have a visiting time. Yes, yes, yes* I can finally meet you after nearly two months. This is the best thing could have ever happened, isn't it?

Seyed Majid called in the afternoon and told Maman that we can go to the Revolutionary Court tomorrow at 3:00 in the afternoon to meet you, but later he called again and changed the time to 10:00 in the morning.

Can you believe it? I know, I know, I can't believe it, either. I still wait for his call to cancel it. It's like a dream which is going to come true. I am so excited that I cannot write. I can't do anything. I have my final chemistry lab exam tomorrow, but this is the last thing that I am worried about now. I want to open my window and shout and tell everyone that tomorrow I see my Baba. I love you, Baba. I can't wait to tell you how proud I am of you and how much I love you. I love you Baba, I love you. I love you times thousands.

I don't know what to do when I meet you. Shall I hug you? Shall I kiss you? Do you think the guards will let us to do what we want? Maybe they won't let us touch you!! And what should I say? Will they let us tell you all the news? Can we take you some food? What do you desire most to eat? What should I wear tomorrow? I think I will wear my school uniform, because after our visit, I must go to school.

Oops, I just looked in the mirror and found a couple of perfectly new pimples on my forehead. They weren't there this morning! Always, right at the important occasions, pimples appear!! What should I do with them now?

Baba, I am a bit scared that tomorrow you won't be yourself. You know what I mean? I am scared that you could say something that we wouldn't expect to hear from you! I better not think about these things. I really cannot write, my mind is chaotic.

Otherwise, I have bad news, as usual, for the end: Maman should have a surgery on her hip. It seems there is a tumor which should be taken out. She has postponed the surgery 'til the end of the book fair.

See you tomorrow.

P.S. It's 2:00 in the morning and I cannot sleep. I've been tossing and turning in my bed for hours, but I don't even feel drowsy. You know, we had a serious family conversation last night. Maman told Mohammad and me that we should tell you all the news. She said even if they cut the visit and threaten us to be silent, we should not stop. "This is the only chance we've had after two months and we should use it to make Baba aware of the happenings outside the prison," she said. Oh, Baba, tomorrow will be a very hard day!! I'll go back to bed to rehearse what I should tell you. Can't wait to see you.

*Wednesday, 9 May, 2001*
*Midnight*

I have a strange feeling. I should be happy, but I feel empty inside! It was a very difficult and emotional day for me, the hardest one during the last two months.

At 9:30, we were at the Revolutionary Court. Without waiting, our pass papers were issued and we headed up to Branch 26 on the second floor. We were silent on the staircase. Maman was in front of us and I noticed how difficult it was for her to take each step; she was in pain. Mohammad and I were following her. This was my first time going up to Branch 26 and for Mohammad, it was his first time in the Revolutionary Court. My heart was beating faster and faster with each step and I don't know if I was excited or scared!

We went through the long corridor of second floor, towards Branch 26. On the right side of the corridor were rooms or entrances to different branches. People were standing or sitting in the available chairs on the left side, facing the branches. Some were in prison uniforms and handcuffs, which made me remember my nightmare about you. I tried to push the negative thoughts away, but then my eyes fell on the prisoners' feet; they wore dirty plastic slippers. I really didn't want to see you like them. It would be so humiliating, and I wouldn't be able to bear it. While passing by the prisoners, I prayed deeply in my heart, "Please, God, please, God, I don't want to see Baba like this!"

We met Mr. Saber's[28] family in front of Branch 26. They were supposed to have a meeting time at 9:00, but apparently he had been late.

At 10:00, Mr. Saber appeared in the corridor with several agents around him. His sons ran to him, and how wonderful was the scene of a father embracing his sons.

Mr. Saber had lost weight and his hair was cut very short, but his smile was the same as before. We all briefly greeted each other

---

28     A member of the *Melli-Mazhabi* Coalition.

as he made his way towards the Branch office, which he then quickly entered. Seyed Majid told Maman that we should wait 'til their meeting finished. That was the worst forty five minutes I've ever experienced.

But, when I saw Mr. Saber, I had felt better, as he was in normal clothes and didn't have handcuffs. But still, I was very nervous. Time passed very slowly and I couldn't stop my mind from thinking about you. I rehearsed the things that I wanted to tell you and tried to keep concentrating on this.

Mohammad was sitting silently next to me, but Maman was in pain and couldn't sit on the chair. She was standing and leaning back on the wall. But both of them were thoughtful! Perhaps, like me, they were thinking about what to do and what to say when we finally get to meet you after *two months*.

Finally, Mr. Saber came out from the branch accompanied by agents. We stood up for him. He paused and told Maman while patting Mohammad's shoulder, "Everything will be solved Insha'Allah." He smiled and then left.

We entered Branch 26. The entrance room to the branch is Seyed Majid's office. There are two other rooms in the branch; one is for Judge Haddad, which, I assume, is where trials are held, and the other room is where we were guided to go.

The room was big. There was a desk and a chair in the right-hand corner, and there were also four chairs in the middle of the room, arranged such that two of these chairs were opposite to and facing the other two. We sat in the chairs, as Seyed Majid told us to, and waited for you.

A young agent came in, a big briefcase in hand. Without looking at us, he sat behind the desk and opened his briefcase on it. I couldn't see inside the briefcase, but I guess that there was a recorder in it to record our voices during the meeting.

I heard you saying hello to Seyed Majid and my heart was close to stopping. I can't describe the moment you entered the room. You had lost so much weight that your clothes were kind of hanging on you. I noticed how you had fastened your belt very tightly to keep your pants from falling down. And your hair was cut very short, like Mr. Saber's. You looked older, as if some years had passed since we last saw each other!

I was the first to run to you and I hugged you as tightly as I could, and when I felt the pressure of your arms around me, I just remembered how much I missed you, so I pressed you harder.

Baba, I have no words to explain that moment; I hugged you, I pressed you, and I kissed you. You hugged me back, you pressed me back, and you kissed me back. I felt I was in heaven. I didn't want to let you go.

I told you, "You've become so thin!"

You smiled at me and said, "I'm more handsome like this, am I not?"

I just stared at you.

After you had hugged and greeted Maman and Mohammad, we sat in the chairs. I sat next to you so that I could hold your hands in mine and Maman and Mohammad sat in front of us.

Seyed Majid was standing at the doorstep and looking at us, but no one paid attention to him. We felt the pressure of being monitored, but at that moment, nothing was as important as talking to you, giving and receiving information.

You started by saying this: "Don't believe these rumors that we're given drugs or injected with them. These are not true." It was obvious that you were told to say this.

I looked at your face. Your eyes were full of tears and your lips were slightly trembling. *What have they done to you?* passed my mind. I was so close to bursting into tears, but I swallowed them and said, "Baba, your students haven't accepted any professor to replace you in their class. They said they won't attend the class if its professor has been put in prison because of his thoughts." Your lips were trembling more than before. You bit your lower lip to hold back your tears. It was the hardest moment of this meeting. Looking at you in that condition was unbearable, but I didn't want to cry in front of the agents. I wanted to show them that I am strong.

Mohammad said, "Mr. Khatami announced his candidacy for the second term of his presidency."

Your eyes rounded and, surprised, you said, "Really?"

Maman said, "The Intelligence Minister has denied your charges and said there is no evidence to show you are subversive." You didn't know that.

Me: "One hundred fifty representatives of Parliament have defended you and rejected the accusation of subversion." You didn't know that.

Mohammad: "One hundred and nine university professors wrote an appeal letter to President Khatami and protested against your arrest and demanded your release." You didn't know that.

Maman: "Your colleagues at the Chemistry Department, in a letter to the Head of Judiciary, have rejected your charges and demanded your release. And the Islamic Association of Students of the science faculty has also protested against your arrest." You didn't know about these.

You didn't even know that nine of your comrades were released on the second day of your arrest and that the members of *Nehzat-e Azadi* were arrested a month later.

You were isolated for two months with no news from the outside. You were even given some false news, and suddenly, we were bombarding you with information that you hadn't expected. I still can't imagine how you felt when you were hearing our news, which carried so much hope. I just saw in your eyes that with each piece of news, you gained more and more power. Then, in one moment, I saw your eyes were shining again.

After successfully completing our mission, it was your turn to give us your news. Honestly, I had doubted that we could talk to you and give you the news that easily. No one stopped us or threatened us! *Big surprise!!* However, you couldn't talk to us freely.

Maman said, "Your face is too yellowish."

"There is not much sun," you replied.

Then Seyed Majid jumped into our conversation and said, "It is prison, but there is no prohibition for exercising and going outdoors!!" You looked at him, but didn't say anything.

"The food is fine, but I eat less," you continued.

"What do you wear there?" I asked. I know it was the most stupid question I could ever have asked, but it just came to my mind.

You said it was "not like the striped prison uniforms, but it's a kind of comfortable pants and shirt."

Mohammad asked about the others and if you had seen anybody there or not.

"No," you said, but then you mentioned that you can hear Uncle Reza's voice when he reads the Quran and says his prayers.

Maman asked if you're aware of your charges. And you said your accusations are being "subversive" and a "member of the *Melli-Mazhabi* Coalition."

You said that after your arrest, they left you alone in your confinement, without any interrogation, for a month!! "They themselves don't believe that I'm subversive. If they did, they wouldn't have left me alone for such a long time," you said. "When my interrogator came to see me after the *Nowruz* holiday, I told him if the matter was not that urgent, why wouldn't they let me be with my family for the New Year? And he just replied that he was sick."

Who knows what you have gone through?! You were alone in a cell with no access to anyone – even an interrogator – for a month! This is so oppressive!

Maman told you about the raid on the magazine's office, and surprisingly, this was the only thing you knew about. You said that this was not the first time in this country that a ruling system felt threatened by a scientific magazine. Then you mentioned Mirza Kazem Khan Mahalati's name and told his story: "He was among the first group of Iranians who were sent to France one hundred and fifty years ago to receive higher education. He studied chemistry and when he came back to Iran, he started publishing a magazine called *Danesh*. He wrote about chemistry and physics in the magazine, but after he had published some issues of it, the king was told that this magazine would be dangerous for the society, so it was closed."

There was sorrow in your face while you were telling us this, as if your magazine would have the same destiny! I told you that we have a stall for *Chemistry & Development* in the book fair to reduce the bitterness you felt from the raid and the shutting down of the magazine, but it seemed that didn't work; you just gave me a pale smile.

Baba, I don't know why I'm describing all these things. You already know everything from our meeting. But I just need to write about it. I need to let the words flow out. I need to review and document everything in order to not forget what happened there. You know what I mean? I just need to write and write and write. This makes me feel better. If this is boring for you, just skip it.

Our meeting lasted for an hour. Time passed so fast. Seyed Majid said, "Time's up."

Then, suddenly, the expression on your face changed to a serious one. "Be careful about your phone calls. Don't offend anybody," you said.

Okay, we got it. Our phone is being monitored. I told you before, I've felt it since your arrest.

We stood up to say goodbye. I grabbed your hand. It was cold, but gentle and strong. You smiled at me. I was ready to give whatever I had to not have to leave you behind there. You told Mohammad and me to study our lessons. "Nothing is more important than your education," you said.

The guy who had been sitting behind the desk closed his briefcase and went out. Seyed Majid came close to you and whispered something in your ear. Then you told us that the conversation of this meeting shouldn't be spread out.

"Baba, you are in prison, and we don't know what is going on with you. We are outside of prison, and you have no idea about the happenings outside, so we will do whatever we think is beneficial for you," I said loudly, so Seyed Majid could hear. I don't know how I gained the courage to say this, but I'm happy I did it. And I saw in your eyes that you were satisfied as well. They should know that we're not scared of them. Don't you agree?

We hugged and said goodbye.

We left Branch 26 while you were still there. I cannot describe my feeling at the moment we stepped out of the Revolutionary

Court. I even can't find a word for it! I just felt something stuck in my throat and I couldn't speak.

Maman and Mohammad went to the book fair, but I had to go to school. On my way, I recalled that I forgot to tell you something. I wanted to tell you at the end that I am proud of you, I love you, and I am waiting for you to come back home no matter how long it will take. I kept it for the end so I could tell you so loudly that all the agents, Seyed Majid, and even Judge Haddad could hear, but I just forgot. I was so overwhelmed that I forgot the most important part!!

At 1:30, I arrived at school. I went directly to the chemistry lab, where the exam was being held. I met Yasi sitting on the floor of the hallway, waiting for her turn for the exam. When she asked me, "How was your Baba?" I burst into tears. I couldn't talk. The only thing I needed was to let my tears come out. They had been trapped in me since morning and I couldn't stand to keep them there anymore. Actually, they had been held back since your arrest.

I was weeping so badly, as if I had lost someone I loved. I couldn't stop it. Even when Mrs. Ghasemian, our chemistry teacher, asked me, "Is it about your father?" I couldn't talk and I just nodded my head.

I did my chemistry experiment perfectly, mixing acids and alkalis, with blurry eyes, sniffling as I breathed. I wrote the result on a paper, which became wet from my dropping tears. Before leaving the lab, Mrs. Ghasemian hugged me tightly and told me, "Since I've found out about your father, I've been praying for him. You should also pray and ask God to help him." I started weeping again in her arms. I noticed her whole body was shaking badly and she tried hard to hold back her tears. I could just manage to thank her for her empathy.

You know, Baba, I've never been like this; crying in public or in front of people is not my kind of thing!!

But, after all, I finally felt kind of better. I stopped crying and I felt some feeling of relief inside after two months. I needed that. I would have preferred it not happen in school, but I don't care anymore. I needed to empty myself, and it just happened.

I don't know when you can read this letter! After one month? Six months? One year? Two years? Ten years? I don't know! But when you reach here, I want you to know how much I am proud of you. I am so proud of having a father like you. Thank you for being my Baba!

Love you so much.

P.S. I just looked at the time: 2:00 in the morning! I feel numbness in the tip of my thumb and index finger from writing so much. *Ten pages*!! It was a long day. A very long day.

*Thursday, 10 May, 2001*
*11:00 pm*

Hello Baba,

Finally, I went to the book fair today. Our stall is very small and simple. Its walls are decorated by the magazine's cover pages, and at the front there is a desk loaded with different issues of *Chemistry & Development* magazine. Tomorrow, I will take some photos for you.

Many people and friends stopped by our stall. Some of your students came and asked about you. They said they've missed you at university. A lady from the University of Zahedan wanted to subscribe to the magazine. I explained to her about your situation and the suspension of the magazine. She got so upset and prayed for you. I gave her some issues of the magazine to read and know how amazing you are.

In the afternoon, Tara came and we went browsing around the fair and bought some books. I bought a book about Hitler and I want to read it as soon as possible. It was written by his lover, Eva Braun. After reading *Man's Search for Meaning*, my mind is kind of engaged with the character of Hitler. I want to know how he behaved with his loved ones and if he was a brutal man with them, too?! I think I could find my answers in this book. I'll tell you when I read it.

I'm sorry, I didn't buy anything for you. I tried to find something, but it's really difficult to buy a book for you. I even asked one of the publishers, "What kind of book would you suggest for someone in prison?" He gave me a strange look. Then I explained to him that you are a political prisoner. His expression then turned friendly, and he suggested that I buy novels which would help to calm your mind. I couldn't make a decision on what to choose for you, but I bought two novels for myself and he gave me a great discount. Are you interested in novels? I haven't seen you read one! As far as I remember, you read books with titles that I could barely even understand!

You know, Baba, I tried not to think about you today. Don't be upset by what I'm about to say, but I wish I hadn't met with you. Before yesterday, I was stronger and more patient, but I don't know why I've become more vulnerable since I met you. I want you to come back home. We need you, Baba. Maman is in pain and needs to have surgery. Mohammad is under a lot of pressure for his entrance exam and I am tired of everything. I just want you back home. When is this nightmare going to end? Do you know?

Miss you, Baba, more than you've ever thought.

*Friday, 11 May, 2001*
*11:30 pm*

Dear Baba,

I wasn't in the mood for anything today. The sky was dark in the morning and later, it was raining cats and dogs. My heart was like the sky all day. I was alone at home, and with every sound of thunder, I cried louder and louder. I think God's heart was heavy, just like mine. We cried together.

I don't know what happened to me after meeting you! My tears roll down my cheeks for no reason. I try to hide this from Maman and Mohammad. In front of them, I am smiling, as if nothing is going on in my heart. I don't want to upset them. But don't worry, Baba. I'll be better. I promise.

Maman said today was very crowded at the fair and that, just like other days, many strangers and friends dropped by our stall. Mohammad bought a book for me: *The Brothers Karamazov* by Dostoyevsky. I am really eager to start reading all my new books, but the final exams will start soon and I am so behind on my studies.

Please pray for me so I can pass them well. I want to make you happy and proud.

I know I'm able to do anything if I really want it, am I not? You always told me and Mohammad this quote from Edison: "Genius is one percent inspiration and ninety-nine percent perspiration." I was in second grade when you wrote it on paper, like an equation, to make it easier to understand: *Genius = 1% inspiration + 99% perspiration*

Do you remember that? To be honest, I barely understood at the time what that exactly meant. You told me, "Look at this paper whenever someone tells you that you can't do something, or when you feel you're unable to do something." You told me I just need to believe in what I want and try hard to achieve it.

This piece of paper has been under my desk's glass top since then, and I've glanced at it for years while I've been doing my homework. Today, when I noticed it again, I just felt your presence beside me, telling me the quote. Telling me that this phase of life will pass soon. Telling me that I should be patient and strong.

Baba, I promise to you that I'll study hard for my exams. I promise to be strong and patient. I am your little girl, and you know how tough I am. I really am, aren't I?

Love you, Baba dear.

*Sunday, 13 May, 2001*
*3:30 pm*

I have something incredible to tell you. You can't believe how helpful and kind people are when they find out you are in prison.

Our insurance plan had expired in March, in the midst of your arrest, and Maman had totally forgotten to renew it. Only when this surgery came up did she find out that we don't have an insurance plan! Oops, I know!!

Yesterday, she went to the insurance office and explained to the manager that she was so preoccupied with your situation that she forgot about the insurance plan and that she needed to renew it. She told him that she has a surgery on the way with no insurance to cover the cost!!

We basically didn't think that they would do anything about this. *But* the manager told Maman that she shouldn't be worried at all and that he would fix it. He just called an hour ago and said our insurance is active from now on and Maman could use it for her surgery.

You see how people are helpful? I know, it's hard to believe!

During the last two months, we faced many stories like this. Several times it happened that taxi drivers who took Maman to the Revolutionary Court refused to accept their fare when they found out about why you are in prison. They told Maman this is the only thing they could do for you.

It's happened twice so far that we have found a packet of money behind our windows from anonymous people. One person had attached a note to the money and introduced himself or herself as your student. "This is my savings. Sorry it's not much, but this is the only thing I have to help support my professor," he/she wrote on that note.

Some of our neighbors are also so kind. They call from time to time or come over to our door to ask if we need anything. They generously cook us food and bring it to us very often.

Did you expect that much kindness and attention from people? It's so touching, isn't it? When I see these things, I tell myself that it is always worth doing anything for your people, for your country. They understand who is right and who is wrong, who tells the truth and who lies to them. People knows these things.

By the way, yesterday, and also today, some other arrestees had visiting times with their families. It seems the Revolutionary Court has also become merciful after two months!! Touch wood!!

A hundred kisses.

*Monday, 14 May, 2001*
*9:00 pm*

Hello Baba,

Shocking news!

Mr. Basteh-negar, in a meeting today with his family, said that his charge is "plotting to overthrow the state" and he faces the death penalty!! *Yes,* I do write correctly. *"Death Penalty"* is exactly what he said to his family.

I got goosebumps when I heard this and even now, as I'm writing, I feel chills all over my back. What is happening there? They want to execute Mr. Basteh-negar?! What has he done? Why they are bothering us like this? They announce the verdict without holding a trial! I should take back what I said yesterday about the mercifulness of the Revolutionary Court.

This morning, Maman and the other women went to Iran's Islamic Human Rights Commission. Mr. Ziaee-far, the secretary of the Commission, told them that his commission is not in a position to do any more for you, as the Judiciary was not responding to his letters. They've never been responsive to anyone! Not to the Parliament, nor the government, and not even to the human rights organizations! So disappointing!!

I'm trying to focus on my exams these days and to not think about bad news. You know, my teachers somehow found out about you and they are so supportive.

A few days ago, Mrs. Fatemi, my Farsi literature teacher, paged me to the school office and asked about you. She told me, "This period helps you to become a stronger and more powerful girl in life. Many people are thinking about your father and they pray for him."

And today, Mrs. Aghaee, my Arabic teacher, just showed up behind me while I was busy writing during the exam. I froze for a second when she tapped my shoulder and asked me, "Do you have any news from your father?"

She is the kind of teacher who likes to control the students. No one can talk without her permission. Any sound or any movement is forbidden in her class. Who dares to do that? When she teaches, her shrill, stern voice can be heard clearly all over the school. Everyone, from teachers to the students, turn silent in awe of her.

She kindly told me, "You have to study hard and this situation should not affect your education." She even gave me her phone number and told me to call her any time I have questions about my Arabic lessons! I couldn't believe she was the teacher I knew before.

You know, Baba, I receive such kindness because of you. People like you and respect you a lot. These happenings make it easier to bear your absence. Believe me!

Miss you, Baba dear!

*Wednesday, 16 May, 2001*
*Midnight*

Dear Baba Hossein,

Today was a bad news day! Are you ready to hear?

Cousin Ali visited Uncle Reza at the Revolutionary Court today. He said Uncle Reza had lost a lot of weight; so much so that he couldn't recognize him when he first saw him.

"He said 'hello' first, and I had to stare at him before it dawned on me that the skinny being before me in the Court corridor saying hello was my father," Ali said. Apparently, his psoriasis has worsened in the prison. Ali said he pulled up his trousers and there were horrible marks and blood clots.

Ali is so worried and anxious. He thinks that Uncle Reza has been brainwashed and was being forced to confess. He said that when he tried to tell him some news from outside, Uncle Reza showed no interest. "He just kept saying 'thank you' to the agents who were standing there and saying that they are so kind to him," Ali said.

My lovely Uncle Reza, what have they done to you? Please be strong.

Uncle Reza said that he is blindfolded in the yard, in the interrogation room, almost everywhere, except his cell. I remember you also mentioned that you're blindfolded during the interrogation, or you have to face to the wall to avoid seeing the interrogators. This is ridiculous! I mean, if they think they are right, then why do they hide themselves behind you? They interrogate you without the presence of your lawyers in an inhumane situation! So unfair!

Baba, I have another piece of bad news for tonight! I know, I'm also tired of bad news, but apparently it is not going to end! I am fed up with bad news!!

The confession of Ali Afshari[29] just broadcasted tonight on TV. It was horrible! He is just a university student! He expressed

---

29    Former political secretary of Daftar Tahkim Vahdat, a student organization in Iran.

his regrets because of his activities, and then he apologized to the Supreme Leader and the people of Iran.

He was arrested a few months before you and now he confessed on national TV. I felt very bad when I saw him in that condition. I don't know if he was forced to do that or if he willingly accepted to do so! In both cases, I think it is not correct to put someone in front of a TV camera and let him or force him to confess against himself. He shouldn't be put in this situation before being tried with the presence of his lawyer and a jury.

I don't want this happening to you. *Please, please, please* resist their pressure. I can stand your absence for years, but confession on TV about something that is not the truth is unbearable! I'm sorry to be so frank. I don't know your situation there and I shouldn't judge if this does happen, but I'm just telling you my real feelings. I would hate to see you confessing on TV. This would be the worst thing that could ever happen in my whole life! Don't do it.

Please be strong.

*Thursday, 17 May, 2001*
*One hour after midnight*

Hello Baba,

I'm terribly sorry that I wrote all that silly stuff about confessions last night. It's just that I had never seen a confession on TV before. It was the first time and I was so overwhelmed. The only thing I thought was, "I don't want to see you in that situation." I was so selfish and just thinking about myself! Please forgive me.

I talked about this with Maman because I felt really badly. She said before the Revolution, political activists were tortured and made to confess. "Some died under torture without opening their mouth, and some couldn't stand it and said what they had been asked to, whether true or false," said Maman. She said that the same thing, more or less, has happened after the Revolution.

I agree with Maman that we should never judge these people. The accusing finger should be pointed at the systems that put people under physical or mental pressure to confess and not at the victims. These confessions aren't valuable, as they haven't been obtained within free and fair circumstances. Am I not right, Baba?

Please forget about what I wrote last night. Do whatever you think is better for you. I love you, no matter what happens.

And now, please listen to an unexpected news! You will be terribly surprised!

Can you guess who was at the fair today? *President Khatami.*

We didn't know that he intended to come. He just appeared suddenly. When Maman heard that he was at the fair, she left the stall to find him.

There he was, standing in front of one of the stalls, some aisles away from ours, talking to the stall holders.

"Mr. President," Maman cried. The crowd didn't let her get closer. "Mr. Khatami," she cried louder.

Just imagine the situation for a second: the president was surrounded by his bodyguards, people, lots of reporters, and photographers. In that bustle, there was no way for Maman to get closer to be heard. But the president miraculously heard her voice. He turned his face to Maman and moved toward her.

Maman introduced herself and said, "Is it fair that my husband, after years of teaching and researching at university, is being kept in solitary confinement?"

"You are right," the president said. You could see the sympathy in his eyes and his voice.

"Wherever we go, no one is responsive. Our loved ones are suffering and so are we." Maman was yelling at him at this point. "To whom should we complain about this injustice?"

Maman's firm voice spread out in that hall. The whole crowd was silent and just the clicks of flashing cameras could be heard. People wanted to know who this woman was; after all, someone dared to yell at the president and the president, with a soft and kind voice, kept saying, "You are right."

Maman told President Khatami that she is so worried about your health and asked him to send trustworthy doctors to the prison to check up on you. "We have no one except you to make requests from or complain to," she said.

"I truly sympathize with you," Mr. President said kindly, and he promised to continue following the case.

After saying, "Thank you," Maman went back to the stall and Mr. Khatami continued his visit in another direction. However, the story didn't end at that point!!

Some minutes later, the president appeared with his usual smile at our stall. It was evident that he came deliberately. I think, through this action, he wanted to show his respect to you and to your work.

Maman explained about the magazine and gave him all the issues in a packet. "Mr. Khatami, this thought has been imprisoned!" said Maman while gesturing to the magazines.

President Khatami signed the notebook we've put on the desk for suggestions and feedback about the magazine. In the middle of an empty page, he wrote, *Wishing you great success and happiness. Seyed Mohammad Khatami. 17 May, 2001.*

All these happenings were like scenes of a movie playing in front of my eyes. Just unbelievable!!

Today, I really admired Maman. I just realized that I don't know her very well! She is so brave and amazing. She was standing in front of the most powerful man in the country (after the Supreme Leader) and wasn't afraid to complain and demand her rights.

Baba, you should have seen how Maman shouted with self-confidence among that huge crowd. I am proud of her and you should be as well. I want to be like her: a powerful, fearless woman who stands up for her rights. Do you think I take after her traits?

*Saturday, 19 May, 2001*
*11:30 pm*

Yesterday was the closing day of the fair. We've passed ten adventurous days! It began with visiting you after two months and concluded with President Khatami visiting our stall.

Unfortunately, I couldn't help Maman that much, but many friends did. Without them, it would have been impossible to run the stall so successfully.

The next plan will be Maman's surgery. She is suffering and needs to have it as soon as possible. She's trying to postpone it, since she is worried about me and Mohammad. It'll be in the midst of my final exams and Mohammad's studies and she doesn't want this surgery to distract us.

Don't worry, Baba, we're trying to convince her that it's not a big deal and that it will be better for all of us if she could regain her health soon. In one or two weeks, she will have the operation. Pray for her.

Today, some other arrestees visited their families at the Court. I think after today's visits, all the families have been to see their loved ones at least once. I'm now waiting for the second round of visits. Do you have any idea when they could happen? I hope we don't have to wait for another two months!

And a heartbreaking piece of news for the end!!

A plane crashed in Sari two days ago, and all its passengers, including the Minister of Transport and his deputies, seven members of Parliament, and some other authorities were killed. It is a great loss for the government and Parliament. It's been so tragic.

Tomorrow will be their funeral. Maman and other families of the arrestees will attend. They specially want to pay tribute to the representatives who supported us after your arrest. May their souls rest in peace.

Love you and miss you.

*Tuesday, 22 May, 2001*
*2:15 pm in the afternoon*

Good Afternoon Baba,

Mohammad and I have both been sick since Sunday. The doctor said it's a virus! I have a bad stomachache and I've thrown up several times. Mohammad was feeling really bad yesterday, but he's better now.

Bijan called a few minutes ago. He said, "I was your father's classmate at the University of Tehran." I think I saw him once or twice before. Isn't he your tall and sturdy friend who laughs loudly? Hahaha, I don't know how to describe him!

Anyway, he said he dreamed last night that you dropped by his house. You embraced each other and cried with happiness. He said, "You should be strong and be proud of such a father." He was so kind.

All your old classmates are kind. They call from time to time, asking about you, even those living outside the country. "Hard times reveal true friends," Maman says. Baba, believe me, you have lots of true and loyal friends.

Dr. Rabani[30] is the best among them. He has done whatever he could to aid your release from prison. He recently wrote a public letter to the Head of the Judiciary, Mr. Shahroudi, demanding your release. He says in the letter that he has known you for more than thirty years, as a classmate, close friend, and colleague, and he has denied the subversive charges against you.

You know, Dr. Rabani was asked to take over your classes at the university, but he didn't accept. None of your colleagues accepted to do that afterwards. In this way, they show their opposition to your arrest.

I don't want to bother you, but you should know this. Maman can't walk properly anymore. She drags her left foot on the ground. She is in lots of pain.

---

30      My father's close friend and his colleague at the University of Tehran.

She talked to Judge Haddad yesterday about her surgery and asked if they could give you a compassionate leave or not. He said he will see what he can do.

What do you think, Baba? They're going to release you? I hope so. If this happens, you could be there for Maman's surgery. The best time to come back home. Maman needs you. Please come back.

I'm sorry, Baba, I couldn't sit any more. I have twisting feelings in my stomach and I need to lie down. I still feel nauseous!!

I'll write you later.

Wednesday, 23 May, 2001
10:30 pm


Dear Baba Hossein,

Today is the second of *Khordad*.[31] Four years have passed since that unforgettable day! I still remember how I was joyfully jumping up and down in front of the TV when I heard of Mr. Khatami's victory in the election. *Twenty million votes*!! Still unbelievable!

I wasn't eligible to vote that time (which was a real pity!) but I'm happy that I kind of helped him to become the president. Don't you believe that I helped? It's actually true.

It seems I have no choice but to reveal my secret activities after four years. I'll tell you, but promise me not to get mad at me, okay?

During Mr. Khatami's presidency campaign, some friends and I stuck his posters on the streets after school. The brother of one of my friends was part of his campaign, and he was our source for the posters. Every morning, my friend distributed the posters among us and after school, we ran to the streets to glue them on the walls.

Everything had been going well, 'til almost two weeks before the election, our vice principal caught us red-handed in the classroom. "Any political activity is forbidden at the school, don't you know this?" she yelled.

"Yes, we do," we said, with weak voices and our heads lowered.

"If so, what are these posters?" she yelled louder.

There was no way to lie and say that we were just looking at them or something! We had tons of posters in our hands and no chance to deny our guilt.

We were temporarily expelled from the classes of that day and we had to stand in the corridor for our punishment. She

31    The Iranian presidential election of 1997 took place on the second of *Khordad* (Persian Calendar), or 23rd of May. It resulted in an unpredicted win for the Reformist candidate Mohammad Khatami.

warned us that next time, she would call our parents! None of us were regretful, though. The only annoying thing was we had lost the posters for that day!!

Do you think we stopped during the following days of the campaign? Wrong. The following days, we hid the posters somewhere in the garden of the house neighboring our school and after school, we picked them up and continued our mission.

Now, do you believe I was active in Mr. Khatami's campaign?

To be honest, I didn't know him at that time. Nor the other girls. We had no idea who the Reformists were and what that even meant, basically. There was no expectation of us to know these things as fourteen-year-old girls! The important things which attracted us to him were his good looks, his smile, and his charming way of speaking. After Mr. Hashemi[32]—the only president we had seen until then—these could be more than enough reasons to attract us to someone like Mr. Khatami. You know what I mean, don't you?

But now, after four years, everything is different. I know him better and I respect him a lot. He has not only improved many things inside Iran but has also changed the western attitude towards us with his idea about "dialogue among civilizations."

You know, Baba, in my opinion, he is the most artistic and poetic president that Iran has had to this day. His effects on media, literature, art, music, cinema, and theatre are undeniable. Aside from these things, his respect towards women and their rights also makes me want to vote for him.

I know he has some weaknesses, especially concerning your case! But I think that it's out of his power. If he could do something to help, I believe he would. What do you think? Maybe I am wrong. You know better than me. I wish you were here and we could discuss some of these things. You always explain things in a way that makes me understand them better. Since your arrest, I haven't had these discussions with anybody. I miss you a lot!

However, to resume, Mr. Khatami—in my opinion—is the

---

32      Iranian President (1989-1997).

president of the people and not power. His respectful and humble behavior with Maman at the fair proves this to me. And I'm going to vote for him. Just two weeks remain 'til the election and I'm really excited about it. This is the first election in which I am eligible to vote, and it's a good feeling to start off by voting for someone I really adore.

Do you think they'll let you vote in the prison?

*Thursday, 24 May, 2001*
*9:00 pm*

Hello Baba,

Guess where am I now? At an altitude of 2800 meters, in a damp hut at Varevasht Mountain. It's raining outside and very cold inside. I am in my sleeping bag, but apparently this spring sleeping bag is not suitable for these conditions.

Sorry for my messy handwriting; I can barely see my words on the paper. There is no electricity here and I'm writing in the dim light of a candle that's on a ledge.

I know, are you surprised? I wasn't supposed to be here, but it just happened. This morning, Mrs. Arab invited me to a hiking program with students of Sharif University. And I couldn't say no. I really need time off from books and happenings at home. And what could be better than hiking?

Mountains make me feel lighter, more energetic, and confident. I feel my lungs absorb pure oxygen (at a higher level than they're meant to), my blood vessels widen as they carry more blood, and my brain produces more happiness hormones while I am hiking in the mountains. I enjoy huffing and puffing when I have climbed up to the summit. No matter how much energy I use up or how tired I get, I feel more alive with every step. This is the unique feeling that I've only experienced in the mountains, and Baba, you introduced it to me at the age of six.

I hadn't yet started going to school when you bought Mohammad and I each a pair of hiking shoes and told us, "We go hiking on Fridays from now on." For years, Friday meant "hiking day" for us, 'til your knee started to hurt and we stopped this routine.

I don't think I've ever told you that at first, I liked hiking because of my new hiking shoes, but then after several weeks, I came to discover more exciting things while hiking, such as making a fire, brewing a tea over it, and making ash-backed potatoes.

The taste of those smoky teas is unforgettable, is it not? I can still feel the heat of the sooty black potatoes that I held with my sleeves to protect my fingers. They were so yummy!

Later, I started liking the mountains because they made me feel powerful, so that I felt I was able to reach my goals and fulfill my destiny.

Ohhhh, how time flies!!!

Baba, I miss you so badly here. I don't know why all these memories just come alive! I am prepared to give everything I have to return to those old days when my joy and happiness were endless and you were there beside me.

Before the dawn, we sat around the fire outside the hut, drank some smoky tea, and sang a song ("The Sea and the Waves") in remembrance of you. As I was sitting there, looking at the flames of the fire and whispering the song with the others, my heart ached with the pain of missing you.

The candle is melting down fast, and so before it goes out, I want to tell you something:

Thank you, Baba, for waking me up early in the morning on weekends, even during hot summers and cold winters, and pushing me to climb while I was tired and nagging you. Thank you for all the unforgettable experiences; their joy will last forever. I still need you in my life for more.

Please come back home. You shouldn't be in prison.

Miss you to the moon and back.

P.S. If tomorrow I conquer this summit, it will be the first time that I will have climbed a mountain that is greater than 4000 meters in height. I'm so excited!

*Friday, 25 May, 2001*
*8:30 pm*

I suppose you want to hear about my climb, don't you? It did not go as I expected. We couldn't conquer the summit; however, the try was enjoyable.

We moved toward the summit at 8:00 in the morning. It had been raining all throughout the previous night and the ground was so marshy. With each step, huge amounts of mud stuck to our boots and made them so heavy. It was slow-going.

However, the beauty of the scenery was so striking that it would be hard to find its equal. The whole area was covered by wild red poppies. I'm not talking of patches of poppies, I am talking about something really extensive; a sea of red.

Slowly, the fog surrounded us from everywhere; this made it hard for us to see and even harder to move forward. Finally, after two hours of challenging nature, Mr. Arab said that we wouldn't climb any further, as it could be dangerous. Just a few meters remained to the summit, but there was no way that we would disobey the leader!

I just arrived home an hour ago. Physically, I'm so tired, but mentally, I'm more alive than any other time. I'll start studying tomorrow and I'll pass all my exams very well. You'll see.

Good night, Baba dear.

*Monday, 28 May, 2001*
*Noontime*

Hello Baba,

After *twenty* days, I finally talked to you last night. I really miss you. Why don't they understand that children miss their fathers? Don't they have children themselves?! Why would it be so bad if you did call us regularly? I will never forgive them.

You asked me to buy a flower bouquet for Maman's birthday, on the 7th of June, on your behalf. I'll do it, Baba. Don't worry about that.

Our biggest concern at this moment is your stomach pain. You told Maman that the quality of your dinners at prison is so low that your stomach cannot tolerate the food. You said that your interrogator agreed that you should have simple food from home for dinner! We are so surprised by this humanitarian action!! So, it seems your problem is very serious for them to have agreed to this! You asked Maman to bring you dates and strained yogurt, which you can eat with bread for your dinners.

Maman said, "A doctor must examine you."

But you replied, "I'm fine. Don't worry."

How can we not worry? What if your stomach ulcers come back? Baba, you need to be away from stress and have a healthy diet, and this just isn't possible for you in your current situation!

Five years ago, when you were diagnosed with peptic ulcers, our food schedule at home had adapted to your diet. Do you remember? We were just eating boiled food: boiled vegetables, boiled chicken, and steamed fish! No spices, no flavor, and no appetizing appearance to the food! Nothing was interesting about our food. But you and Maman kept saying, "It's healthy. Many people would envy us for having a meal like this." Seriously?

I always blamed you for our being sentenced to boiled food!! But I didn't mean it. I am ready to have boiled food for all my meals with no complaint, if you could just come back home.

I am serious. I just want you to be healthy and to not experience any pain.

Now, listen to this: yesterday was Mr. Khatami's first interview on TV for the presidential election. He looked upset and worried during the interview. In one part of the interview, he said, "In the past four years, my colleagues and I passed through a tunnel of crises. I don't want to explain, but I have two points to make: firstly, I tried to prevent turmoil in the country, as our society needs peace. And secondly, I tried to stay loyal to the people and to not lie to them," said the president.

I believe him that he hasn't lied to the people. What do you think? I wish you would come back home so that we can vote for him together.

Otherwise, I'm thinking to write a letter to Mr. Khatami about you. What do you think? I might wait 'til after the election. He must be so busy currently.

Take care, Baba.

P.S. Maman made the most delicious strained yogurt you will eat. I tried some and it's so tasty; it's made with dried mint and some other herbs inside. Tomorrow evening, you'll be served this delicious homemade strained yogurt. Enjoy, dear Dr. Rafiee!

Tuesday, 29 May, 2001
Midnight

Dear Baba Hossein,

The only sound I can hear right now is the chirping noise of the refrigerator. I didn't realize before how its sound is so noticeable at night! I can't sleep. I am worried about tomorrow.

This evening, Maman was hospitalized in room 238 at Atiyeh Hospital and tomorrow morning, she will have a surgery. When you called yesterday, we didn't tell you about the surgery because we didn't want to worry you. Judge Haddad did not grant you compassionate leave, as expected. However, Maman told Seyed Majid the time and place of her surgery when she brought your food to the Revolutionary Court this morning. He promised to take you to the hospital after the surgery to visit her. Sorry to say this, but I don't believe him!!

This is the first time that neither one of you are at home. Without you and Maman, "home" has no meaning! It's just soulless and cold! I've never felt as lonely as I do tonight.

You know, Baba, saying goodbye to Maman was the worst and hardest moment I've ever had. She hugged me and Mohammad so tightly, while crying. She didn't want to leave us alone. I told her that everything is going to be okay and she will back home very soon. But she was so sad.

I held back my tears in front of her, but now I'm crying. I couldn't hold them back anymore. Why do all these things happen to us? I want to study for my exams and not worry about anything else, just like my friends, but I can't. You are in prison and Maman is in the hospital. Nothing is normal in our life!

I'm trying to be strong and not cry, but maybe I'm not the same girl who is sitting here crying. I can't bear to see any more oppression, injustice, and pain! Still, I cannot deceive myself about what I am seeing. The sorrow is too much for me to even try to stop the tears. There are no answers for these tears. Do you have them, Baba? Do you know why we are in this situation? If you know, please tell me.

Baba, I need to talk to you. I need you to hold me in your arms. I need you, Baba. Where are you?

Pray for Maman.

*Wednesday, 30 May, 2001*
*6:30 pm*


Hello Baba,

Mohammad and I just got back from the hospital. Maman is fine. She has some pain, but don't worry, the doctor said that it's normal after the surgery. Many dropped by the hospital to visit her, except you. I knew that they wouldn't bring you! Mohammad says maybe you will come tomorrow, but I'm not that optimistic!

Baba, have you heard that God tests the most those whom he loves the most? God loves Maman the most. Don't you agree? I don't know what else could cause her situation to be harder than it is.

To be honest, if I were her, I would doubt God's justice. But I've never seen Maman complain about any of her difficulties. She always says these are trials from God to test our faith. "We should be patient and trust him. When the time comes, he'll solve everything," says Maman.

I hate to see her in the hospital bed. It's hard to endure this situation without you. I'm sure Mohammad suffers more than me. He doesn't say anything, but I can see the pain and worry in his eyes. He has the most important exam of his life in a month's time and everything has become so complicated. I wish you were here. We both feel so lonely!


*Midnight*

I just watched Mr. Khatami's promotional message on TV. I recorded it for you.

Baba, do you remember what I had told you about the day he declared his candidacy for the presidential election? His short emotional speech from that day was in the message, too. He had said, "The decision to stand again was tough, but I just came forward for the people. The election will show whether the people want me or not, and whatever the people want is final."

He was trying to hold back his tears and that made me remember you, and how you were when we had our meeting.

He paused several times during his speech, bit his lip, and then continued talking as his lips and voice trembled.

Who said men mustn't cry? Even the presidents have the right to cry, sometimes. I wish I had 30 million votes I could give him all at once.

The family, Tehran, 2000

Playing Setar, Tehran, 2000

High school graduation, Tehran, 2001

My mother, *Chemistry and Development* magazine's stall, Book fair,
Tehran, 2001

President Khatami talking to my mother, *Chemistry and Development* magazine's stall, Book fair, Tehran, 2001

*Melli-Mazhabi* Coalition members, first meetings after their release, 2002 (*Left and right images*)

With my father, Road trip to my father's hometown (Birjand),  The Lut
Desert, 2002

With my brother (Mohammad) and my mother, Road trip to my
father's hometown (Birjand), The Lut Desert, 2002

My Parents, Chabahar, 2002

With my parents, The Mausoleum of Omar Khayyam, Nishapur, 2003

Talking about my father in prison, Rally of Amnesty International,
Toronto, 2016

My parents, The day my father released from hospital and detention, Tehran, 2016

# JUNE

Dear Baba Hossein,

I meant to write to you sooner, but I can't seem to find five consecutive minutes to spend in my room. This is a short note to tell you that everything is fine at home.

Maman was discharged from the hospital on Thursday and we received a huge amount of visitors on Friday. It was like the first day of the New Year. Every one dropped in with flower bouquets and boxes of pastries. So many people came over that one of the neighbors thought that you were released!!

Maman is much better now. She can walk, although she still can't sit comfortably. The tumor was benign, so there are no more worries.

Thank you for calling her today. She was waiting for you. You said that your interrogator hadn't told you about her surgery. I knew it. "He told me today and let me call home," you said.

I can't imagine how hard it was for you when you heard about her surgery, but it was good that they at least let you talk to Maman.

I haven't updated you on my final exams lately. So far, so good! But the most difficult ones are on the way. I have a chemistry exam in three days. Hopefully, I will find some time to study. Fingers crossed.

Love you, Baba.

*Monday, 4 June, 2001*
*11:00 pm*

Baba,

I am sooooooooooooooooo angry!

No one is thinking about me! I have an exam tomorrow and the women are still having their meeting here. I haven't finished my chemistry book yet.

Don't people understand that I have an exam? However, this is not just about other people; you and Maman are guilty, as well, for putting me in this frustrating situation.

I am studying in my room, focused on my reading; then, Maman calls me from time to time to serve the guests! And you, whenever you call, you tell me, "Study hard. The only thing you should be doing is studying." Seriously, Baba? How can I study? Please stop telling me to study, because it's impossible!

I don't forgive anyone, neither the Revolutionary Court nor you, Maman, or others. Everybody is trying to ruin my future. If I don't get good marks for these exams, I won't be accepted into a good college, and then I can't go to university. All my dreams for the future will be ruined!

Why does nobody understand my situation? I need *peace* please, please, please…

P.S. (Tuesday, noon) My chemistry exam was terrible. I was so stressed last night, and I couldn't sleep properly at all. I woke up at 4:00 this morning to do some revision, but it was fruitless. This is not my way of studying at all! Over the past eleven years, I had always been completely prepared for my exams and I would confidently walk into the exam room. But today, I lost all my self-confidence!

After the exam, I walked back home alone and thought to myself, "How can I deal with this chaos in my life?" You know what my conclusion is? I won't care about my marks anymore. I'll do my best for the next exams, but whatever happens is fine.

Sometimes things are out of your control, so trying to have control over them just bothers you. I think it's better to accept things as they are. I have accepted this now and I am not agitated any more.

*Friday, 8 June, 2001*
*9:30 am*

Good morning Baba,

It's Election Day!

Mohammad has already gone to one of the polling stations along with some other *Melli-Mazhabi* families. They decided to vote together at the same station. Maman and I will go to a closer and less crowded one, as Maman still can't stand for long.

Before I leave, let me tell briefly about the news.

On Wednesday evening, we held a small birthday party for Maman. As I promised, I bought a bouquet of red roses on behalf of you. We didn't expect you to call, but apparently Maman's situation softened your interrogators' hearts and they let you call us more often! You told Maman that you wrote a letter for her birthday. Is that right?

I'm curious about what you wrote in the letter. Why don't you write a letter to me? Do you know how many letters I've written to you by now? Fifty-seven. But you've never answered any of them.

You asked us to bring your ID card so that you can vote. But the Court was closed on Thursday and this means that unfortunately, you cannot vote. However, I doubt that you could vote today, even if you had your ID card! They wouldn't bring any mobile ballot box into that secret prison. And furthermore, they don't want more votes for Mr. Khatami. Am I not right?

I'm going to the polling station now. I'll write you later.

*10:00 pm*

Finally, I voted for the first time. I am happy and proud. What do you think; will Mr. Khatami get more than 20 million votes? I'm waiting for the results impatiently.

All the stations were crowded. Mohammad said they waited for three hours in line 'til their turn came and they could vote. Even the small station close to our house was busy. We waited an hour for our turn. There were so many young people voting for the first time, just like me. Whomever I talked to had decided to vote for Mr. Khatami.

I enjoyed the process of voting. When the officer applied the ink to my finger and gave me the ballot, I felt like I was the most important person in the world! I know, it's funny, but I really felt like that. I wrote "Seyed Mohammad Khatami" on my ballot paper and cast it into the box. The feeling was indescribable.

*Oh*, I forgot to tell you something. Mohammad said a reporter from Channel Three interviewed him at the polling station. The interviewer asked him, "Why are you voting?" and do you know what his answer was?

He said that he is going to vote to push back those who are against democracy and freedom. "There are many people who are imprisoned because of their thoughts. I will vote to change this situation," he said. I am proud of my brave brother. But I don't think they'll broadcast his interview on national TV. No way!

The 10:30 news is on now. If I get any news about the election, I'll update you on it.

Saturday, 9 June, 2001
11:10 pm

Hello Baba,

I have some good news and bad news!

Good news first: Mr. Khatami won the election! Horrraaaaaaaaaaaaaaaaay!! We won, Baba!

According to the latest news, he got nineteen million votes, but they are still counting the ballots. Hopefully they'll pass twenty million.

People are celebrating this victory; I can hear the sound of car horns in the street. Unfortunately, I cannot join because *I have an exam to study for!* You see what an unlucky girl I am? But not to worry, there's just two more exams left: biology on Monday and geology next Saturday.

Now, the bad news is that Uncle Mehdi Khan finally found out about your arrest. I know, you didn't want that to happen. Our family and relatives all tried hard to hide it by telling a series of lies. But last week, one of his neighbors in the village heard about you on Radio BBC. He then ran to Uncle Mehdi Khan and disclosed the truth without thinking for a moment. I can't understand what he was thinking? What kind of idiot tells bad news so directly to a seventy-five-year-old man? Thank God Uncle didn't have a heart attack!

He called us later and asked me about you. I, unaware of what had happened, lied to him again and said that you are on a work trip. However, he then talked to Maman, revealed that he knew about your arrest, and asked us why we hadn't let him know. He said, "I'm coming to Tehran very soon." Maman insisted that he not bother himself by coming here, as he couldn't do anything, but he said, "I should come." And tomorrow, he will be here.

Maman wants to request a meeting time for Uncle so he can see you. Do you think they will allow it?

*Monday, 11 June, 2001*
*6:40 am*

Good morning Baba,
*Three months* have passed!

It's hard to believe that I met with you just once during these *ninety days*. I miss you more than you can imagine. But I feel I am more patient now! Or perhaps it's better to say that I'm thinking more realistically now.

I have been through a lot. And I just realized that when you face a crisis, at first you feel that it is too much to bear and that it couldn't get any worse. You become distressed and anxious. But then you face yet more problems and that makes you angry. So, you keep asking yourself and asking God, "why me?" But after more and more problems emerge, there comes a point when you tell yourself, "Okay, this is my reality. It's better to accept it as it is and to live it."

I'm at this point. I really want to rise above this crisis and face it with courage and live according to the saying: "I will find a way, if I can't do that, then I will make a way." But if I can't, I just shrug my shoulders and laugh at this unfair world! Seriously, this is my new character.

I had started this letter to tell you about the final vote count for Mr. Khatami, but I took another direction! Anyway, he received 21,654,320 million votes, which is almost eighty percent of the votes. Isn't that incredible? I hope he gains power by this amount of support and continues his reform activities. I hope he can help with your release.

I'll write to you later. I should go to school now. This biology exam is waiting for me!

*7:30 PM*
Hello again,

The exam was fine, I guess. However, the definition of fine is now different for me than before!

I forgot to tell you that Uncle Mehdi Khan is here. He arrived last night. He is so sad and shocked. He constantly shakes his head and says, "Why has this happened, why has this happened, why, why…"

I feel terribly sorry for him. I wished he had never known about your arrest.

This morning, Maman went to the Revolutionary Court to bring your food and also ask for a meeting. She explained to Judge Haddad that Uncle Mehdi Khan has recently found out about your arrest and has come to Tehran from his village, which is a thousand kilometers away, to visit you.

Judge Haddad said he would call tomorrow and say if the meeting is possible or not. He also told Maman that everything will be clear by Thursday. "Some will be released and others will be transferred to the Evin Prison," he said.

You know, Baba, I don't believe him. He always says the same thing, but nothing happens. Last time, he told Maman that after two weeks, everything would be solved, but three weeks has passed and nothing has changed. I don't know why they do this to us? Giving false hope and promises to people is so immoral and inhumane. They are playing with our feelings.

P.S. I read your letter. I know it was for Maman, but as the interrogators, Judge Haddad, and Seyed Majid read this letter before passing it to Maman, I thought it would be so unfair if I didn't!

It's difficult to write a letter to your wife when you know that many strangers will read it, isn't it? If I were you, I would never have written it. I wouldn't like strangers reading my private letters. But you are my lovely, kind, and brave Baba, and you did it for Maman. You thanked her for all her support and apologized to her for all the problems. She needed to read your sweet words. This letter is definitely the best birthday gift Maman has ever received from you.

*Tuesday, 12 June, 2001*
*3:30 pm*

Hello Baba,

Have you heard the news?

Just now, Seyed Majid called and told Maman that Uncle Mehdi Khan can meet you tomorrow morning at 10:00. Maman asked him whether it's possible that we meet you as well. He paused for a second and then said, "Yes, yes. You can all come and we'll figure something out then."

I have a strange feeling! I should be walking on air hearing this news, but I'm not. There's a part of me that impatiently wants to meet you, but another part doesn't. I miss you and you know that. I'm ready to give all I have to be with you (even if it is for a few minutes), but our last meeting was so painful and distressing. I don't want to experience it again. I don't want to see you like that again. I don't want strangers to stare at us and listen to our conversation. I don't want to go to the Revolutionary Court. I hate that place!

Do you mind if we talk about something else other than tomorrow's meeting?

I woke up at noon today. After several sleepless and stressful nights, I enjoyed sleeping in. My last exam is next Saturday; geology, my favorite subject!! (Dear God, please help me to study this boring book. Amen!)

When the exams are over, I will focus on my university entrance exam for next year. You know, I finally made a decision about my major at university: medicine. I want to become a doctor, *but* not a normal doctor! I intend to join Doctors Without Borders. Have you heard about this NGO? I recently read an article about them in a newspaper. They do lots of humanitarian activities in war-torn regions and poor countries. And, two years ago, they received a Nobel Peace Prize for these activities.

Working for this organization would be the most fantastic future I could ever imagine for myself. With this, I can fulfill my two biggest wishes in life: to travel around the world and visit different nations, and to help people in need, alleviate their suffering, and save lives.

I have just one year to put all my efforts toward making this happen. I'll study hard and pass the entrance exam for medical school. I'm so serious about it.

Maman is happy with my decision. What do you think? I wish I could talk to you about this tomorrow, but we will have too little time and there are more important things to tell you!

See you tomorrow.

*Wednesday, 13 June, 2001*
*5:10 pm*


Dear Baba Hossein,

I'm writing this with a heavy heart. Every time I come to the Revolutionary Court, I feel that I have become somehow older and more weary. I lose my spirit and liveliness.

I wish I could cry when I meet you, but I can't. I feel something in my throat and I can't let my tears go. It hurts, Baba, it hurts so badly. But you know what is more painful? Seeing tears welling in your eyes. You, like me, don't let them fall free.

Why? Why don't we hug each other and cry freely? Perhaps you don't because of us, and we don't because of you! This is painful.

We were at the Court on time at 9:30. We sat on the chairs in front of Branch 26, waiting for you. You were late. Very late. I couldn't sit. I had butterflies in my stomach. I walked down the corridor, but very soon I regretted it. Prisoners, handcuffs, shackles, desperate faces… I didn't want to see any of those. I went back and stood next to Maman.

She was sitting sideways on the chair, putting all her body weight on her right hip, trying to avoid any pressure on the left side where she had had the surgery. She was talking to Uncle Mehdi Khan. About what? I don't know. I wasn't listening to them! I just noticed that Uncle Mehdi Khan was shaking his head and mumbling something every now and again.

Mohammad was a few seats away from us, leaning forward with his elbows on his knees. His head was down and his chin rested on his interlocking fingers. He was slightly tapping his toes on the floor. He was probably thinking about the subjects he could have finished reviewing in these past hours.

Baba, do you know about the "*golden time*"? It's a term used for the month before the university entrance exam. Educational counselors say this is a crucial period to review the subjects and avoid any distractions.

Mohammad was literally wasting his golden time at the Court while other competitors were studying. I don't know how he focuses his mind after each meeting and concentrates on his studies again! I should ask him to teach me. If this situation continues, I must learn how to handle it.

Finally, you arrived at 1:00 pm, after a three-hour delay. The meeting was held in the same room as the last time, but there was no sign of that guy with the briefcase. And nobody sat there to listen to our conversation. I thought they might have changed their attitude, but I was wrong. I didn't know something worse was waiting for us!

You were worried about Maman. It was clear from the first moment that something had happened. You told her, "Don't sign any statements!"

"Why, Baba?" I asked. You oddly smiled and didn't say anything.

We told you the news of the election and other things. You talked with Uncle Mehdi Khan and everything seemed to be going well, 'til that telephone call.

Seyed Majid came inside the room and asked Maman to pick up the phone at the big desk! We all looked at him with wonder! Who wants to talk to Maman? I was confused.

Maman picked up the phone and I saw the color of your face change. Your face went red! Totally red. I knew that something was going wrong.

Maman didn't say anything and was just listening. After a few moments, suddenly, she yelled, "Do whatever you want. I am not scared of you. If you want to talk to me, ask to see me next time." I got chills all over my back. She hung up the phone and asked Seyed Majid, "Who was he?"

I haven't seen Seyed Majid look as flustered as he did in that moment. He became pale and agitated. "Nobody, nobody. Don't worry about him. I'll solve it," he said and left the room.

I looked at you. You were pursing your lips. Maman said, "He threatened that he would arrest me if I continue advocating for you."

You said that he was your interrogator and he has told you the same thing.

The situation was nerve-wracking. Why will they not leave us alone even for a minute?! Was this a family meeting or an interrogation session? We finally met you after a month. Would it be too much to ask to meet you in peace?

I tried to say something to change the atmosphere in the room. I told you, "Baba, don't worry. They won't do anything to the families of the arrestees."

You gave me another strange smile, and I now know what it meant. You said, "No, it's not that simple, hon." I froze.

Seyed Majid came in again and asked you and Maman to go to Judge Haddad's room. I was so nervous, as were Mohamamd and Uncle Mehdi Khan. I couldn't process what I had just heard and seen! I still can't understand why all these things happened?!

We heard you yell at Judge Haddad, "My interrogator showed me a warrant with my wife's name. He threatens me by saying that he will arrest my wife and destroy my family. What do you want to do with us?"

Maman was also yelling, "I haven't done anything wrong and I'm not afraid of imprisonment. Tell him not to threaten me and my family again."

I felt chills all over my body hearing your conversation. My hands were cold and shaking. I folded my arms tightly across my chest to avoid Mohammad seeing my hands shaking.

Judge Haddad reassured you that if anyone were able to imprison Maman, it would him, but that he doesn't intend to do this. Both of you came out of that room with worried eyes.

I hugged you for the last time in the corridor before you left. When you hugged Uncle Mehdi Khan, you told him, "I'm sorry for all the pain this meeting has caused you." You left and I saw how he was struggling to hold his tears back.

I looked at you 'til you disappeared at the end of the corridor. You turned your face back several times, smiled at me, and waved your hands. I wanted to run after you. I wanted to tell you, "Don't go, Baba! Come back home with us!" But I just stood in that damn corridor like a statue, looking at you and waving my hand to you. I let you go! What else could I do?

This meeting was worse than I expected. It was a disaster! We came to meet you for some relief, but we all left with lumps in our throats. I can't stop thinking what will happen if they arrest Maman. Baba, I'm scared.

I wish we hadn't had a meeting and that none of this had happened! I can't forget these days and I can't forgive those who caused it. I know you wouldn't agree with the latter. You always repeat this quote of Mandela: "Forgive, but do not forget." But, I can't. At least, at the moment, I can't. Maybe one day I could find a way to forgive them, but not now.

Be strong, my dearest Baba.

*Sunday, 17 June, 2001*
*Midnight*

Hello Baba,

I'm sorry that I didn't write to you sooner. After Wednesday, I sat on my bed and tried to start a letter several times, but I couldn't. I still couldn't digest what had happened that day. My mind had somehow frozen. Imagine how I studied geology in that condition! Lack of concentration added to lack of interest, and you can guess what the result of that was, can't you?

I'm better now. Exams are over and I feel as if a great weight has been lifted off my shoulders. The only thing I need is to relax for a while, fix my bike, and start cycling like every summer.

As usual, I have disappointing news for you. It really grieves me to write bad news over and over, but I promised myself to write everything to you 'til your release, as long as it takes.

After the presidential election, the Article 90 Commission was supposed to present their report on the violation of law in the arrest and detention of the *Melli-Mazhabi* members at one of the open sessions of Parliament. However, today, the women in a meeting with this commission found out that some of the commission's members did not agree to do this. And can you guess who those members were?

I'll tell you: Mrs. Jamileh Kadivar and Mr. Mohammad Reza Khatami! I know, it's shocking and disappointing. I thought they were our allies, but apparently they're not! They argued with Mr. Ansari Rad, who is the head of the Commission, and didn't let him present the report!

Even Mr. Bourghani told the women yesterday, "Why do you want to meet President Khatami? Don't bother him."

Seriously? Are we the bothersome ones, or those who don't carry out their duties properly? Those commission members were holding a report in their hands that indicates you are completely innocent and that your arrest and detention has been a violation of law, but then, they refuse to read it in an open session of Parliament! I can't believe them.

Seems they've forgotten their promises to the people about defending their rights. They've forgotten their duty, which is implementing the law, not acting against it!

I hate politics. It's too dirty. You must be a liar and hypocritical as a politician.

Baba, I hope you get released soon. They are sacrificing you in their games and struggles.

Didn't I tell you before?

P.S. Breaking news: tomorrow afternoon, I will go to the University of Science and Technology. Guess what? The Student Association is going to hold a big ceremony to celebrate President Khatami's victory in the election. They also intend to honor the political prisoners, and for that, they've invited all the families of arrestees to their ceremony. Maman couldn't go, as the doctor has forbidden her to sit or stand for a long time, but she let me attend this ceremony on behalf of our family. Isn't it exciting?!

*Monday, 18 June, 2001*
*Midnight*

I suppose you impatiently want to hear the news of today! I know, I'm thrilled to tell you all the details.

In the morning, I was a little hesitant to go to the ceremony. Maman wouldn't come, and I had no idea what it would look like and what would happen there. But then I told myself, "This is a unique and unrepeatable experience in your life. Let's do it."

Do you care to know how I dressed up? I'm not picky with clothes, but this event meant a lot to me. It was in your honor and as your daughter, I wanted to be perfect.

After trying on several outfits, I reached a combination of green and white. I wore my pistachio green manteaux with a brand new white scarf and milky white pants. Very simple, but different from the university dress code! I wanted to be different.

The ceremony was in the main amphitheater of the university. It was so crowded; all the seats were full, and the students even sat on the steps of the aisles. Many were standing at the back where the entrance was.

Someone at the entrance asked my name. I said that I'm the daughter of Dr. Rafiee. He welcomed me and asked me if I had come alone. Apparently, he didn't expect a teenaged girl to come to the ceremony on her own. "Yes," I answered. He smiled and asked me to follow him through the crowd.

He opened the way and I passed through the people to the front. Everyone moved aside and looked at me with praise and respect. It was the first time that I was treated as a VIP at an event. The feeling was awesome!

I sat in the second row among the other families. I turned back to look at the crowd.

*Wow*, it was incredible! Believe me or not, there were six hundred or more people in that place.

Mr. Tajzadeh[33] was on the stage giving his speech. I was so excited that I couldn't listen to him. I just remember his last sentence: "It shouldn't just be the Conservatives who are reforming their activities; we, the Reformists, should start reforming ours as well."

The crowd applauded as he was coming down from the stage.

The presenter stood behind the microphone and said, "The families of political prisoners are our guests here." He named you one by one and the crowd burst into applause and cheered after each name.

He explained that the security forces of the university, before and during the ceremony, had threatened to shut down the ceremony if any family members of the political prisoners spoke out on the stage! But, he asked the families to come up on the stage and take the certificate of appreciation that they prepared for us.

He named the families of the arrestees one by one and each went up to the stage and received the certificate of appreciation from a member of the Student Association while the crowd applauded.

"The family of Dr. Rafiee," the presenter called your name. I could only hear the sound of applause in my ears.

I had never received so much applause from an audience when standing on a stage. I was so excited, nervous, and flustered at the same time. I received your certificate of appreciation and faced the crowd. Too many people were staring at me and applauding for me (in fact, you). I felt my heart pounding and my feet were totally numb! I didn't know what to do to thank them. I bowed to the crowd. The sound of cheering rose.

All the families were on the stage and the presenter was talking in honor of the political prisoners, when suddenly the microphone was cut off!! The security forces couldn't tolerate our presence on the stage!

However, the crowd's reaction to this was brilliant! They stood up and started applauding. I can't find the words to explain the moment! For several minutes, I only heard the continuous sound of applause and cheers. I wish you were there and could see it with your own eyes.

---

33    Political Deputy Minister of Interior (1997-2001).

The only disappointing part was that Mr. Tajzadeh had left the ceremony after his speech. He was supposed to come up onto the stage and hand the certificates of appreciation to the families, but he decided not to do so. Maybe, like the MPs, he also thought it would be better not to interfere in your case?! You know politicians!

After the ceremony, the members of the Student Association invited us to their office. There were about sixty students in that tiny room. They asked us to talk briefly about your situation.

As the women were speaking, I was thinking whether I should say something as well. I wasn't expected to do so and I hadn't even prepared anything to say. I prayed in my heart that they wouldn't ask me to talk. Seriously, I was flustered.

I was the youngest in that room and obviously the last one to be noticed. One of the students said, "Do you want to say something about your father?"

I paused for a second, breathed out, and said, "First of all, I'd like to thank you for all your support. This ceremony means a lot to me. It gives me an enormous amount of hope to know that people care about my father and that they have not forgotten him. My father is a great man. He shouldn't be in prison. He's been trying to improve his country and make life better for the people. This is not a crime! I'll choose his way in my life, because I have faith in him and his thoughts."

Everyone was silent and stared at me for a second. Then one of the students started to clap his hands and the others followed. They told me that what I had said made an emotional impression on them.

What do you think, Baba? Do you like my short speech? Please consider that I was unprepared and these words just came to my mind impromptu.

Today was one of the best days of my life. I experienced all of these things because of you. Baba, you made me so proud today. Thank you a thousand times over for all the things you give to me, even when you're not here with me.

I love you to the moon and back.

*Wednesday, 20 June, 2001*
*5:30 pm*

Hello Baba,

The calendar shows that a *hundred days* have passed since your arrest, but to me it feels like a *hundred years*!

Last night, the women had a meeting at Mr. Basteh-negar's house. I attended their meeting again after a long time. They'd divided into two groups and were arguing for two different plans for today. One group wanted to go to the Revolutionary Court and meet Mr. Mobasheri, the head of the Court. But the other group thought that these meetings were useless, and they wanted instead to stage a sit-in in front of the UN office in Tehran for some hours.

Maman was in the former group. She tried to convince the women to attend the meeting. She said, "We could always stage a sit-in in any given place, but after three months, we have finally been given this appointment at the Revolutionary Court. This would be a chance to talk to the head of the Revolutionary Court in person. He is the one who was in charge of all these arrests and detentions. So, it's better to use this opportunity to first talk to him, and then if it doesn't work, we could do other things."

The other group was reluctant to come. They said, "Now it's the time to do something more noticeable to put pressure on the authorities."

Anyway, after a long argument, neither group could convince the other. And therefore, each group decided to follow its own program.

I have no news about the sit-in program, but I can tell you what happened at the Revolutionary Court. Mr. Mobasheri told the women that, very soon, in one or two weeks, the situation of the arrestees will be clear.

I know. The same promises as before! Days pass and the only things we hear are false promises. It's hard to believe them after all those promises that were never kept, but there is no other alternative. We must be hopeful, Baba! Hope helps us to be strong and to continue our fight.

Be hopeful!

*11:30 pm*
Baba, I wrote a letter to President Khatami on behalf of Mohammad and myself. He is going to Mashhad tomorrow and many reporters, including Cousin Ali, will accompany him. Ali said he will give the letter to him on the plane.

I attached the draft version to this letter. Let me know what you think of it.

*Dear President Khatami,*

*Please accept our warm congratulations on your victory in the presidential election. We apologize for bothering you at the beginning of your trip, but we have nobody else to write to.*

*A hundred days have passed since that night that we cannot forget. That night, we did not understand what was happening and did not know why our father had been arrested! It's still winter and cold in our home since our father's arrest, and spring won't come unless our father comes back and brings his warmth back to the home.*

*Mr. Khatami,*

*Our father is our teacher. A teacher who taught us to observe well, listen well, and speak well. He taught us to defend our rights and fight against falsehood. He showed us the oppression and injustice in the world, and beside it, he showed us the kindnesses and goodness that exists, too. He taught us to know God and pray to him, how to love and be loved. He taught us how to support our country's interest and how to work to improve our country.*

*He would drive us from village to village, from one city to another, and from one province to the next, all over Iran, to tell us why he loves this country. He took us from the Anahita Temple to Tchogha Zanbil, from Persepolis to the Chehel Sotoun Palace, from* the greenness of the North to the ruins of the South, from the Shrine of Imam Reza in the East to Abidar Mountain in the West, to teach us that we must respect all cultures, languages, and religions.

Our father taught us many things, and for a while now, he has been teaching us how to be patient. And what a tough and overwhelming lesson it is!

Would you please tell us how we should accept that our teacher has gone wrong? How we should believe that our father has made a mistake? No, we cannot accept any accusation against our father. We are proud of him.

Mr. Khatami,

We've passed the toughest time of our lives over the last hundred days. The oppression and injustice that we have faced is unforgettable. If you would grant us the permission to meet you, it would be a respite for us from our hurt.

Sincerely yours,
Mohammad and Maryam
(Children of Dr. Hossein Rafiee Fanood)

*Thursday, 28 June, 2001*
*4:45 pm*

Dear Baba Hossein,
I'm sorry that I'm not very consistent with writing these days. I'm rather worried and that makes it hard to write.

You called on Monday and asked Maman, "Why did you go to the University of Science and Technology?" Maman said that she didn't go there. It was me, Baba. I went there.

Then you said, "What about the UN office?" and Maman denied this one as well. You told her that your interrogator said that she must write a statement and deny that she had gone to these places, otherwise she might be arrested!

I know you are under pressure and this is so annoying and painful! This is torture! They threaten you by saying that they'll arrest Maman. The thought of you being troubled so, even for a minute, is unbearable. Why does this nightmare never end?

Maman didn't write the statement because she thinks this is what they would want, to manipulate us. She says, "If I accept to do this, then other things will follow." She's decided to firmly resist their orders.

After your call on Tuesday night, when Maman was coming back home from the women's meeting, she saw a stranger's car parked in front of the entrance to our apartment building. There were three men standing outside the car, chatting and smoking, and one sitting in the driver's seat. "They looked like the Revolutionary Court agents, with untrimmed beards and loose shirts untucked over their pants," said Maman. She became suspicious but avoided drawing attention to herself.

She passed the guys and as she entered the building one of them said, "Excuse me, Ma'am, do you know Mr. Rafiee in this building?"

Maman, very coldly, said, "Sorry, I am a guest. I don't know anybody here." Then she came in and shut the door.

This is so suspicious! We don't know if that was a show or if they really didn't know Maman. But, in both scenarios, they wanted to scare us, and I am really scared. Maman didn't tell Mohammad, but as I'm going out a lot, she told me, so that I'd be careful about strangers and not talk to them.

I don't feel safe anymore. I take peeks through the window several times a day to see if there is a suspicious car or person outside our apartment, and when people ring the doorbell, I first look through the window to see who they are!

Baba, I'm scared of a raid on our house and Maman being arrested in front of my eyes. I don't know what I would do if this happened.

They are torturing us by threatening to arrest Maman. Why do they do this? I can't understand them. Maman hasn't done anything wrong, she has only been defending your rights.

I wish you would come back home soon, and that all these nightmares would end.

Love you, Baba.

# JULY

*Sunday, 2 July, 2001*
*11:20 pm*

Hello Baba,

I'm not feeling well writing this letter and I know that you are not feeling well, either; I felt this from your call this evening.

Every time I hear you voice, I become…! I don't know what I become! Happy or sad? I don't know, Baba. I really don't know.

You pretended to be fine, but I sensed from your voice that you were not. I know how your voice sounds when you are happy and when you're upset. I sense when you are under pressure. I feel it, Baba, even if you don't say it.

You know what Judge Haddad told Maman when she brought your food to the Court yesterday morning? "Mrs. Rafiee, you would be more patient if you knew how much better it is for Mr. Rafiee to be here! He's become disburdened from all his wrongful activities!" He spoke as if you are guilty and being in jail is redeeming you from your sins! But what sins? What guilt? Is telling the truth a sin?!

Maman just told him, "You and I know that my husband is innocent and hasn't done anything wrong. It's better to free him as soon as possible and end this injustice."

Baba, we don't have any power. They do! They have the power to oppress us. They have the power to threaten us. They have the power to accuse us. They have the power to tell us whatever they want. But we don't have the power to confront them. I'm sorry that we cannot do anything to help you. I am sorry, Baba. We do our best, but it's nothing in comparison to their power.

Maman says that our activities will bear fruit and that we just need to be patient.

"Oppression won't last forever," she says. Maybe she is right. Mandela was finally released, after 27 years! So please be strong and keep up your hopes.

I miss you, Baba. Miss you a lot.

P.S. I forgot to tell you that I got my marks. They are not really bad! They're better than I had expected. Chemistry: 17.25/20. Biology: 18.25/20. Geology: 16/20. Arabic literature: 19/20. And I got 20/20 in all the other subjects. My average grade for this semester is 18.66/20. It's not that bad, is it? I should start searching and applying for a college.

*Monday, 3 July, 2001*
*1:30 am*

Dear Baba Hossein,

I can't sleep tonight!

I've been writing to you for a long time, now. I write to you about what I'm doing, where I'm going, what I'm reading, how I'm feeling, and almost everything else about myself. But you haven't told me anything.

I want to know, what does your cell look like? What do you do to pass the time? Do you get bored? Do you get depressed? What keeps you from losing your mind?

You've been in solitary confinement for one hundred fourteen days! *One hundred fourteen days!* How do you spend all the hours of solitude? No one to talk to and no one to listen to! If I were you, I would have become crazy by now!

Last night, after your call, I couldn't sleep. I lied down on my bed, going over my thoughts. You might have two to four hours of interrogations a day and a half-hour walking in open air. In all other hours of the day, you are in your cell alone. What do you do there?

I tried to imagine!

Your cell is very small, maybe three meters by four meters. There is a bed with a hard mattress, a blanket, and a pillow. There are no windows and no natural light. A fluorescent light is overhead, turned on at all times. Is it like this?

During the first few days, you might have spent your time by reading all the writings and carvings on the walls. Previous prisoners wrote their names, poems, quotes, and the calendar dates everywhere. You might have made up stories about these people in your mind. And then later, you began scratching tally marks on your cell wall to count the days.

You sometimes put your ear against walls to try to hear sounds from the next cells. Once, you had mentioned that you could hear Uncle Reza's voice as he is praying. Sometimes, you tap on the wall and wait for a response, then you may hear someone is tapping back. You try to whisper something like, "I'm Hossein, who are you?" Then you press your ears to the wall, waiting for an answer. You may or may not receive an answer. I hope you do.

Sometimes, you might crouch down by the food slot at the bottom of your cell door and try to look outside or listen to the sounds. Can you see something, Baba? Maybe just a beam of light!

When you come back from interrogation sessions, you're pacing back and forth across the longest possible diagonal of your cell. How many steps is it? Maybe three or four? You're muttering and moving your hands in the air while pacing your cell – like the times when your mind is busy with something.

You do exercises like pushups and sit-ups. You count them every day and try to increase the number by practice. How many can you do in a minute, now? Twenty? Maybe more!

You might sometimes lie on your back, stare at the light on the ceiling, and make up stories. About me, Mohammad, and Maman. Thinking about our memories, our trips, and our home. You miss home. Don't you?

You try to eat as slowly as you can. Eating is the best way for killing the time. You try to chew each mouthful twenty times. When we were kids, you always told us to count how many times we chew each mouthful; I would never even reach ten times.

For dinner you, have bread and strained yogurt, some nuts, and dates from home. I can clearly imagine how you break off a piece of bread, grab a generous mouthful yogurt with it, and take it to your mouth. You chew twenty times. It tastes like home, doesn't it?

Baba, I try to soothe myself by making up these stories every night. I try to convince myself that you are doing fine there. But the truth is more grievous than these stories. The truth is that solitary confinement is torture, and nothing is fine with that. Maybe its effects are not as visible or tangible as physical torture, but this doesn't change the truth.

All the families are concerned about this situation continuing. It seems the authorities are not willing to end this. All our appeals to the Judiciary, Parliament, and government have so far been fruitless. So, in the last meeting, the women decided to write a letter to the European Parliament and ask for international attention and help. Maybe this will work.

Baba, be hopeful and strong. Everything will be fine. I promise.

Take care.

*Friday, 7 July, 2001*
*10:45 pm*

Hello Baba,

Finally, Mohammad took his university entrance exam this morning. He said it was fine. And I really wish he gets a great result. He deserves it. He studied through a tough time, in all the difficulties at home, and never complained. He's been so patient and strong for me and Maman. I'm so proud of him and you must be, too!

Otherwise, the countdown has just started for me and this makes me nervous. I know, I should start planning and studying for next year's exam. But first off, I should make my decision and choose a college.

The good colleges are so expensive, and I'm really apprehensive about them. Maman tells me not to worry about the tuition fee, but I cannot be indifferent. Your salary hasn't been stopped yet, but who knows how long it'll continue to be paid? If Mohammad cannot make it to go to the public universities, then he should register for private ones, and that means heavy tuition fees!

I don't want to add more burdens onto Maman's shoulders. I am smart and hardworking and I could pass the exam, even if I study in a normal college that is free to study in, couldn't I?

By the way, the landlord of the magazine office has asked us to vacate the place. Maman and I have been busy with packing up, cleaning, and moving in the last two days! It was tough to empty the office without you. As I was packing, I recalled the first day I came to the office; I went from one room to the other and told you how to decorate them. I never thought that one day we would vacate the office without you.

Baba, you will publish the magazine again. Everything will be the same as before. Maybe even better.

Just keep your hopes up.

*Monday, 9 July, 2001*
*Midnight*

It was an unexpected meeting! Seyed Majid called last night and told Maman that we could meet you today. Surprise!!

As usual, we arrived earlier than you, and Seyed Majid asked us to wait for you inside the room. He had become so oddly friendly! He stayed in the room 'til you arrived and constantly talked with us.

You know, he's totally changed during these four months! When I saw him for the first time, he threatened Maman in front of my eyes, and yesterday, he was sitting in that court room and chatting with us like an old friend! He might have forgotten those days, but I never will.

I didn't feel comfortable talking to him. I preferred to wait for you in the corridor. I tried to avoid any eye contact with him and limited my answers to his questions to a simple "yes" or "no."

He patted Mohammad on the shoulder and asked about his exam. Then, like an uncle to his niece and nephew, he began advising us that we should just study and not to pay attention to anything else! "Really? Before the arrest of our father, we were just studying!" I didn't tell him this, but I wish I had.

Mohammad's face was indifferent. He didn't feel easy in that situation as well.

Thank God you came on time, otherwise he would have wanted to sit and continue his artificially-friendly chat!! I'm not mean and I'm not rude. I really don't need their friendly behavior because *they are not our friends*. I just want them to release you and end this ridiculous situation!

You'd lost more weight since last month. But you insisted that you were fine.

The first thing you said after greetings was that you were forced to talk in front of the camera. I got a sinking feeling in my stomach!

"Was it an interview?" Maman asked.

You said, "No, I was alone. I just talked about the *Melli-Mazhabi* Coalition and our activities for about twenty minutes or so." You said that your interrogator threatened you to do this, saying that otherwise, he would keep you in solitary confinement for another six months and would arrest Maman, too.

"Were you allowed to speak freely or were you told what to say?" Maman asked. She was trying to understand what had exactly happened. I was amazed by how calmly she talked to you. Mohammad and I were kind of frozen; we stared at both of you and waited for the end of the story.

"I just told the truth. And this made my interrogator angry. He wanted me to express regret and remorse for my activities, but I didn't do that," you said.

I breathed out at this moment.

I'm sorry, Baba. I know I told you that I would be fine with whatever happens, but I think I'm not. When you were telling this story about being forced to speak in front of a camera, I realized that I'm not ready for any kind of confession or repentance. I don't want to see you on TV. I'm such a coward and a selfish girl, I know, but at least I'm honest!

You seemed to deliberately raise your voice so that Judge Haddad and Seyed Majid could hear you from the other room. "After four months, they haven't found anything to hold against me, so they're trying to extract a false confession and make me repent. This will never happen." You said the last sentence with a solid voice.

Baba, I can feel how much you struggled with yourself about what to say to help yourself and Maman. I can imagine that you didn't sleep the night before the filming, turning and tossing in your bed, pacing in your cell, and thinking, "What to say? What is correct to say?" You might have thought about saying what they wanted to release yourself and prevent Maman from being arrested! But you didn't do that.

Thank you for resisting their unfair demand. I'm sure you're going to win this battle of right against wrong. They will never win.

The meeting was too short. We didn't have enough time to talk about other news. We hugged each other and said goodbye. We left you behind in that Court again.

All the way back home, we sat in silence in the car and just listened to the tape of one of your favorite symphonies: Beethoven's Moonlight.

Listening to symphonies was boring for me before, but I enjoyed it today. You know, Baba, I've changed a lot since your arrest. Don't you believe it? I started liking whatever you like. Now, I read your favorite newspapers and listen to your favorite music. This helps me to feel that you're here beside me.

I wish you could have a cassette player in your cell. Can you imagine how Tchaikovsky, Beethoven, Bach, and Mozart could give a soul to that soulless prison? But even without a tape player, it's still possible to feel their music. Try this: lie down on your bed, close your eyes, and listen to the music playing in your head; *Da-da-da-DAH... Da-da-da-DAH...* Can you hear Beethoven's fifth symphony?

When we arrived home, I couldn't go inside. I took my bike and went out. I pedaled and pedaled and pedaled, as fast and as hard as I could. I cried riding my bike as the wind scattered my tears in the air. I wept and pedaled 'til sunset.

When will this nightmare end, Baba? When?

*Friday, 13 July, 2001*
*2:30 pm*

Dear Baba Hossein,
*Four months* have passed!
That night, when I heard you were arrested, I didn't become upset. Instead, I was excited that I could experience new things. It's a shame, I know. Who becomes excited about her father's arrest? I was so naïve and stupid. I didn't know what awaited me in the next months. However, now, the only thing I want is an end to this bitter experience. I want you to come back home and for everything to become the same as before. Is it possible, please?

Since the exams, I entertain myself by reading books and cycling. Both of them disconnect me from this world and let me plunge into my dreams.

Do you want to know what books I've read by now? *The Unbearable Lightness of Being,* by Milan Kundera; *Gone With the Wind,* by Margaret Mitchell (the novel is way more amazing than the film); and *Love is Eternal,* by Irving Stone. I put myself to sleep every night pretending I'm the main character of the book I'm reading at the moment. Can you guess who I am now? Djamila Boupasha.

Yesterday, on your bookshelves, I found this old-looking book about Djamila Boupasha, written by Simon de Beauvoir. When I started reading, I couldn't put it aside. She was such a strong and dauntless woman, wasn't she?

When I get tired of reading, I go cycling. This is my lifestyle now: read, read, and read, then pedal, pedal, and pedal. In between, I eat and sleep.

I've always wanted to be the first Iranian woman to win a medal in road cycling. I know, I don't have a chance, since women cycling is still forbidden in this country and there is no team to join and practice. However, when I read the story of Lance Armstrong, I become more determined to follow my dream.

Have you heard of him? He is an American cyclist; he beat cancer few years ago and then got back to cycling again. He won the Tour de France for two consecutive years. Everyone says he will win this year as well.

He is my role model now.

There are unfair laws, thoughts, and judgments against women in Iran, but I should never lose hope. I'll live my dreams, and hopefully one day, my dreams will come true. Until then, I'll continue cycling in the streets and imagine myself as one of the Tour de France competitors who beats everyone and wins the yellow jersey.

You didn't know how extremely dreamy your daughter is, did you?

Miss you, Baba.

*Monday, 16 July, 2001*
*11:30 pm*

Hello Baba,

I'm officially a college student!

Last week, I visited some colleges and finally, I made my decision; I enrolled in one close to our house.

The college is now holding a summer school for six weeks, three days a week. It's basically for reviewing the main subjects of high school: math, physics, chemistry, and biology. The classes started a week before and I'm kind of behind, but no worries. I can catch up on them.

There is a quote written on the college office wall: *Successfulness is not reaching the end goal but is the persistent forward progress*. I agree with that. I have a tough year ahead and no one knows what will happen by the end of the year. I just need to put all my mind and efforts on my studies, move forward, and not think about the endpoint.

Baba, do you believe that the universe returns back to you the same kind of energy you put into it? I do. From now on, I will become a totally optimistic girl and I'll repeat positive sentences in my mind, like *I can pass the exam; I can enter medical school; I will become a doctor; I'll go to deprived villages, to Africa, to war-torn regions, and help people in need*.

Now, I should go back to do my assignments for tomorrow.

Love you.

*Thursday, 19 July, 2001*
*5:30 pm*

Baba,

Is this real, or am I dreaming? I can't believe it. I was jumping up and down crazily for a minute when Maman said the news. This is the best thing I have ever heard. You are not alone anymore. It's unbelievable!

Maman was at the Court today and Judge Haddad told her that now, you and Dr. Maleki are in the same cell. OMG, my hands are shaking as I'm writing this. I still think it's a dream, and when I wake up, it will disappear!

Finally, solitary confinement has ended. Horraaaaaaaaaaaaa-aaaaaaaaaay!! Everyone who heard the news burst into tears. I'm so happy for you, because now you have someone to talk to, listen to, and share your feelings with.

I have many questions: "How were you feeling when they took you to this new cell? Was Dr. Maleki there already, or he was brought to the cell after you? What did you do when you saw each other?" I want to know all the details. Why don't you call home and tell me that this is real and it's not a dream? I need to hear this from you.

I can't write anymore. I'm going to call everyone and tell them this incredible news.

Finally, I have good news to share.

*Monday, 23 July, 2001*
*3:45 pm*

Hello Baba,

Since I heard that you are no longer in solitary confinement, I feel like a heavy weight has been lifted off my chest. I know, you are still in prison, but having someone with you in the cell after four months of solitude is a miracle. Since then, I wanted to do something to tell God how I am grateful for this happening. And you know what I did?

I went to Rofeideh Nursing Home Care this morning. It's a residence for physically and mentally disabled children. One of my friends in my *Daf* class is doing volunteer work there and a few days ago, he asked me and two other friends to join him and play music for the kids. I told myself this is the way I could thank God. Without any hesitation, I accepted.

Before going there, I was a bit nervous. I've never played for disabled children and I didn't know what their reaction would be. Or how I should behave with them. But all my worries were groundless. When we started playing, they came close to us and started dancing, happily shouting, jumping up and down and spinning around us.

When we were done, they ran to us and hugged us! One of them threw herself into my arms and tightly hugged me, as if she knew me for ages!

Their teacher said that most of them were abandoned by their parents. And that they are thirsting for kindness and pure love. This is very sad! They are small kids deprived from their parents' love. I cannot understand how people could do this!

Baba, after a long time, I feel I did something useful. It's not just me; the other guys also have the same feeling. We all decided to continue performing there as volunteers 'til the end of the summer. Next week, we'll take extra *Daf*s and drums with us and let the kids play with them. I already miss them all!

When you are released, I'll take you there. You should meet these little angels. They make friends with everybody in the blink of an eye.

Sunday, 29 July, 2001
5:45 pm

We haven't heard from you for a week. Maman took your food to the Court this morning. She made it double, as Dr. Maleki might like to taste some homemade food after a long time.

Seyed Majid said that you will call tonight. I miss you, Baba, but talking on the phone doesn't help. Even meeting you in the Court is not helpful. I want you at home. I want to talk to you about my new plans, dreams, and decisions without the fear of anyone eavesdropping. I hate the feeling that all of my private life is being monitored by anonymous people!

Everyone keeps silent about you. President Khatami is silent and doesn't speak out. He hasn't even answered my letter! The MPs haven't yet presented the report of your arrest. I don't understand what they are waiting for! You are innocent and still in jail. How could they keep silent? Why they are so indifferent?

Politics is the most horrible and dreadful thing in the world!

By the way, I received my college uniform today, and I must wear it in September. The color is something! I mean, it's weird, I don't even know what to call it. It's like a combination of wheat and peach! I know, it's terrible. I think they've intentionally chosen this awful color to make us look ugly so that no boy looks at us!! This color automatically repels all the boys. Believe me!

Apart from the uniform, so far, I like the college, my classmates, and the professors. Some of the girls are really smart and I try to group and study with them.

There is one more thing I like about this college and it's the cozy juice shop next to it! It's the first place I go after the classes with the other girls. Don't laugh! I'm in love with its fresh icy pomegranate juice! The best summer drink I've ever tried. I'm kind of addicted to it. When you get released, I'll take you there for some and you'll see I'm right.

Baba, this is not fair. You no longer know where I'm studying, what I'm wearing, where I'm hanging out with my friends, and many other new things about me! I'm scared that this will continue for a long time, and one day, you will know almost nothing about me! I'm really scared of that day.

I wish you could read my letters!! You know, I'm still hiding them in the freezer. I've frozen them for a day in the future when I can hand them to you. When will this day come? Nobody knows. I'm scared that one day, all of the freezer will be filled with my letters and you won't have come back.

But don't worry. I'll continue writing to you, telling you everything. I will never stop. I promise.

I miss you, Baba. I miss you a lot.

P.S. It's already midnight and you didn't call! But guess what? Lance Armstrong won the Tour de France. I told you he would win, didn't I? Maybe next year, we can go to France together and watch the competition closely by following the riders at each stage. What do you think?

# AUGUST

*Friday, 3 August, 2001*
*Midnight*

Hello Baba,

Right now, I'm the happiest person in the world!

Yesterday, you called and said you and Dr. Maleki are now in a bigger cell with four of the other arrestees. I can't believe that after all those tough days, something like this could have ever happened!

(Thank you, my dear God! Thank you for your kindness. Thank you for not forgetting us.)

You are happy together and so are we. Mrs. Emrani invited all the families of the arrestees to their cottage in Karaj. It is a very nice place, far from the city and in the middle of the gardens and farms. We went there yesterday afternoon and just returned. So refreshing!

It was the first time after your arrest that the families gathered together with happiness and joy. Although some of you are still in solitary confinement, and no one knows what awaits you in the future, this news has at least given all of us some hope.

Last night, we stayed awake 'til morning. We were playing, singing, laughing and having lots of fun. In the morning, some went walking in the gardens and some (like me) swam in the pool. Everyone relaxed and stopped worrying about you for a day. All of us needed this vacation, no matter how short it was.

The women, especially, deserved some time off. They've been fighting for your rights non-stop during the last one hundred and forty-five days. (Can you believe today is 145th day of your detention?) They've met many authorities or written letters to them. They've constantly interviewed with the media and have never been silent about you. Their courage, will, and attempts to releasing you are commendable. Don't you agree?

I cannot keep open my eyes anymore. I'm too sleepy.

Good night.

*Sunday, 12 August, 2001*
*10:30 pm*

Dear Baba Hossein,
*The fifth month!!!*
The pain of missing you is always alive in my heart.

I'm sorry that I'm not consistent with writing these days. I'm so occupied with studies. This summer school makes me crazy! I go to college every other day, and on days off, I do lots of assignments. It doesn't look like a summer at all! Am I complaining? Mmmm, not really! (Maybe a little!)

Before your arrest, I thought that Iran was on the path to further development, especially after Mr. Khatami became president. However, now, I'm pretty sure that we are a backward country, very far from democracy and development. It's a shame that they've kept innocent people in prison for five months without giving them access to their lawyers and without holding a trial.

You are not criminals, you are being denied your basic human rights because of your belief in tolerance, pluralism, and democracy. (I copied this sentence from the letter by the families to the European Parliament. And it was well-said!)

After five months, they couldn't prove their accusation against you, but then, why don't they release you?! *Why?* No one is even responding to us.

Sorry, Baba, I didn't want to vent my frustration and anger on you! I'll end this letter here before I become even more angry.

Good night.

*Monday, 13 August, 2001*
*Midnight*

Hello Baba,

You won't believe this: Cousin Ali went to the Revolutionary Court today to meet Uncle Reza, but Seyed Majid said that his meeting has been postponed to Wednesday. Then—listen here—he told Ali that Maman, Mohammad, and I can also come to the Revolutionary Court and meet Uncle Reza on Wednesday!!!

They generally give meetings to immediate relatives and I don't know why they granted us such a big favor! Do you have any idea?

I'm happy and sad at the same time. I'm always feeling like this when I'm supposed to go to the Revolutionary Court. I love to meet you, or Uncle Reza, but then I hate the place and the atmosphere.

I haven't seen Uncle Reza for five months (just once, in my nightmare!) and I'm worried that he is not the uncle that I once knew! I don't want to see his pain and distress. I can hardly bear yours. I cannot witness this situation again and again and again. The truth is that I really don't want to go there, but I'll go because of Uncle Reza.

Why is life so very difficult, Baba? Why?

*Wednesday, 15 August, 2001*
*Midnight*

Dear Baba Hossein,

I'm totally broken. I had a tough day at the Court. I hate that Court. I hate it. I never want to go back there again.

I wished I hadn't met Uncle Reza. The person we met was not my lovely uncle!

When I met Uncle Reza, I couldn't recognize him! He had lost lots of weight, his face had turned yellow, and all his skin – those parts that we could see – was red and scaly, due to his psoriasis disease.

He hugged me and kissed me. I was so close to bursting into tears. I tried to hold them back, but my lips were trembling and I couldn't speak. I was stronger before in these situations, but I think I'm gradually losing my energy and strength.

Uncle Reza looked at me and, with a shaking voice, told me, "If you cry, I'll cry too, darling!" I held back my tears but something was stuck in my throat and I couldn't say a word 'til the end of the meeting. My eyes, ears, and throat are still aching.

What did they do to my dear Uncle Reza? His hands were shaking and he was so strangely silent. Cousin Ali and Maman talked to him, but he just listened and said nothing. At one point, he said, "I was very sick for a while; one night, Seyed Majid brought a doctor into my cell for me. But I'm fine, now." None of us believed him. He was not fine! I don't know why they still keep him in solitary confinement.

Oh God! Why do good people always suffer? Tell me, for what reason should he be in that situation? Why don't you do anything to end this oppression?

Baba, sometimes I don't understand God! Where is his justice?! If you understand him, if you have answers for my questions, please tell me.

Today was the worst day of the last five months. Even worse than that day when we had a meeting with you for the first time, worse than that day Maman had a surgery, and worse than that day I had a chemistry exam and couldn't study! It was such a horrible day. When will these bad days end? When?

When we arrived home, I couldn't hold my tears back anymore. I felt if I didn't let them go, I would suffocate. The only place I could hide and cry secretly was the bathroom. I got into the shower and sat under the falling water. I cried and cried and cried until I could cry no more.

Baba, I can't. I can't continue this. I'm broken. I'm exhausted. This is too much for me. I don't want to come to that Court again. It is a torture to see the pain, stress, and suffering of your loved ones and not to be able to do anything for them. This is torture for me. I can't do this anymore.

Please come back home! I am begging you. Please, please, please.

*Thursday, 16 August, 2001*
*Midnight*

Hello Baba,

Seyed Majid called this morning and told Maman that they want to bring you home on Friday for a family visit. This is now their new show!

On Tuesday, they brought Mr. Emrani to his home, along with lots of Court agents. And tonight, they brought Dr. Maleki to his son's engagement ceremony. Maman was there. She said, "Everywhere you looked, you could find an agent. Some stood in the street, some in front of the doorway, in the staircase, and even inside the apartment, where the ceremony took place."

It was good that at least they let Dr. Maleki attend his son's engagement ceremony, but by sending dozens of agents, they just ruined a familial and private ceremony. Nobody felt comfortable! Maman said most people were crying instead of laughing!

I don't want to think that this situation might happen to me or Mohammad in the future. It would be my nightmare if one day I get engaged and you are still in jail. *No, no, no…* This won't happen. Promise me, Baba, that you will be released soon and will be beside me in all my life events. Promise?

I don't want these agents to come to our home and search my room, but at least it's better than meeting you at the Revolutionary Court. I hate that place.

Are you excited to see home after five months?

See you tomorrow! Hopefully this meeting goes calmly at home.

*Friday, 17 August, 2001*
*10:00 pm*

Baba,

Why didn't you come?

I expected you all day. I baked you a chocolate cake. I asked Maman to cook cutlets, your favorite meal. I dressed up and waited for you for hours; I was sitting on the sofa and I did nothing except peep through the window from time to time to check whether you had arrived or not! But you didn't show up.

They didn't bring you and they didn't even call. What do they think about us? How could they ignore our feelings so easily? Maybe they assumed that instead of hearts, we have stones in our bodies! Could they, themselves, stand to be away from their parents or their children for more than a week? No, I don't think so. If they experienced it once, they would treat us differently.

They have no idea about what we've been through during these five months. Could they understand how it feels when you have no news from your father for months? When false accusations are broadcasted publicly against your father and he is not able to defend himself? When you are scared to turn on the TV, lest you see your father confessing in front of the camera? When your father is in jail while your mother goes under the knife in a hospital? When your brother has the most important exam of his life and nobody is there to support him? When you graduate from high school and your father is not there? When you sleep every night with the fear of a raid on your house and the threat of your mother's arrest?

They don't understand how it feels when you've been waiting for hours and hours to meet your father after *forty days*, but nobody brings him!

I don't want to write a word about these days anymore. I wish I could bury all the memories and never recall them. I feel desperate, lonely, and lost in this unfair world. I feel incapable of doing anything.

Baba, please come back home.

P.S. (Saturday – Midnight) Maman went to the Revolutionary Court this morning. She was so angry about yesterday. Seyed Majid told her that you would be released very soon, and that's why they decided not to take you home for a visit. Do you believe them? I don't. They always play with us. And I am fed up with their games.

*Monday, 20 August, 2001*
*10:30 am*


Good Morning Baba,
Guess what?
Maman is in the headlines of today's newspapers. All wrote about her courageous talk with the president at Parliament. And even some friends called and said that they heard her voice broadcasted on VOA radio.

Here is the headline of one of the papers: "Hossein Rafiee's Wife Demands Justice From the President." This is another one: "Khatami to Hossein Rafiee's Wife: You Have a Right to Shout. I'm Here to Listen to You." There are a lot. You should look at the essays. I'm so proud of Maman.

All this happened by coincidence. The Article 90 Commission finally presented their report regarding your arrest last week, in an open session of Parliament. Yesterday, the women went to Parliament to follow up on the results of their objections to the Article 90 Commission. And Mr. Khatami was also there to introduce his new cabinet to Parliament.

Maman seized the opportunity again and turned to speak to him. In front of many journalists, reporters, MPs, and ministers, she addressed the president: "Mr. Khatami, we are tired of this oppression. Please do something to end this situation. Why should our loved ones still be in prison? Why don't you do anything?" and so on.

Maman was yelling at him and the whole time, he silently stood beside her and the other women, just listening!

In the end, Maman apologized to Mr. Khatami that for having raised her voice, but you know what his reaction was? He told her that she had a right to do so! This was the second time that he treated Maman so respectfully. Although we all know your situation is out of his hands, he tries to do whatever he can, even if it is just listening to the pleas and complaints of the families of the arrestees. I'm happy that I voted for him. I am, I really am.

Baba, did you know that Maman has no fear of anyone? During the last six months, I saw her yelling at many authorities, from Seyed Majid and Judge Haddad to MPs and the president, demanding her rights in situations that I can't even imagine myself being able to stand firmly, let alone being able to say a word! She has a powerful charisma that enchants everyone. This is a new thing I've found out about her after your arrest.

*7:30 pm*
Mr. Emrani has been released!

I'm afraid that maybe I'm dreaming! But this is not a dream. Yesterday, the Court asked Mrs. Emrani to provide bail. She was told that Mr. Emrani might be released today or tomorrow! And this really happened.

My hands are shaking and I can't stop crying, but I must write this: *Baba, you will be released soon as well.*

You called in the afternoon and told Maman to prepare a bailout for the Court. When she hung up the phone and said the news, we both burst into tears. This was the first time that we cried freely in front of each other. We don't need to hide our feelings anymore. We don't need to pretend that everything is okay, because everything is going to be okay very soon.

I was sitting on the kitchen floor, weeping like a kid. I couldn't stand up. I was pouring out all the pressure of these months. Poor Mohammad! He had just arrived home and saw me in that situation. I couldn't talk. I laughed and cried all at the same time. Maman told him the news and I saw how his eyes lit up.

Baba, I can't do anything. I've lost my concentration. I can't believe this. Many things have happened these past few days, and I have not yet fully understood and absorbed their reality. I'm too amazed, excited, bewildered, and happy at the moment. I don't know what to do!

I can't wait anymore. I want to write about your freedom in my next letter.

See you soon, at home.

*Tuesday, 21 August, 2001*
*10:30 pm*

Hello Baba,

Did you sleep last night? I didn't. Not a single wink. I don't think I can sleep tonight, either.

Maman presented the bail to the Court this morning and completed all the legal procedures for your release. She met you there. She said you've lost more weight since the last visit and you had a toothache. No worries, you are coming home. You'll be fine very soon.

Why does time pass so slowly? I can't sleep and I can't even eat. I have a fear that something may happen and you won't come back home. But I won't let this fear overcome me. Whenever I feel it, I repeat my positive sentence in my mind: "Baba is coming home soon! Baba is coming home soon!"

This will be the longest night ever. I decided to read a book, but I couldn't concentrate. I opened the book and read a page, but then my mind wandered somewhere else. I started this letter an hour ago, but it seems it's not going to be finished tonight!

You know what I'm daydreaming about the most? The moment you walk into the home. I've dreamed about this moment over and over again over the past months. Every time, I add new details. It's like a movie scene that I've never gotten tired of watching.

Baba, please excuse this being short. I can't write anymore. I want to lie down on my bed and just dream about the moment you step into the home.

Love you and impatiently waiting for you!

*Wednesday, 22 August, 2001*
*One hour after midnight*

Dear Baba Hossein,
Welcome back home!
Today was the most wonderful day that's ever happened. You arrived home at 4:30 in the afternoon.

When the doorbell rang, I shouted, "Baba's arrived!" I was so excited that, really and truly, my feet would hardly take me up from the chair to the door phone. I answered and said, "Yes?"

"Anna, tell Maman to come down to the entrance of the building!" It was your voice. I can't find the words to describe my feelings of that moment.

Maman signed the papers of the Court to confirm that you were brought home. I was hiding behind the wall, stealthily looking at you while you were talking with the agents.

When they left, I couldn't stand anymore. I ran to you and I threw myself into your arms. "Baba, you finally came back home!" I whispered in your ear. And you just pressed me harder in your arms.

Many called and many dropped in to meet you. It was like *Nowruz*! But no, this time was different. This time, you were at home and hosting the people. The scent and sound of happiness and joy are everywhere. Hugs, tears, laughter, flowers, chocolates, and sweets are endless now.

I wish these things will happen at the others' homes as well. Two other arrestees were also released after you this evening. And hopefully, others will be freed very soon. There is no reason to keep them in jail for any longer!

Baba, I have many things to tell you. Your absence was quite long. *One hundred and sixty-four days!* I can't summarize all the happenings in a day, or even a week. I don't know how to start! Maybe the best way is to give you the letters. What do you think?

I took all the letters out from the freezer. I'm sitting now on my bed and they're all in front of me. Everything is in these letters. All my feelings, all the happenings, my dreams, successes and failures, almost everything from these six months.

This will be the last letter. As I promised, I continued writing 'til you came back. I can't believe this finally happened! You are at home, safe and sound. However, many things have changed. I'm not that girl from six months ago. I grew up in different ways. Your detention has totally changed my visions, goals, and dreams about the future. It was a tough time, but I believe this period was necessary in my destiny. It opened my eyes to a different world!

We still don't know how this story is going to end. You are released on bail and have a trial ahead. But I don't want to worry about it. You are home now, and this makes me feel secure.

It's time to deliver the letters to their recipient. Take your time. There is no rush to answer eighty-three letters!

Good night, my dearest Baba Hossein.

# EPILOGUE

On December 1, 2002, Hossein Rafiee was tried behind closed doors. The charges were: plotting to overthrow the State with acts against national security; spreading propaganda against the State; inciting and seducing people in order to undermine the security of the State and create violence; encouraging students to challenge and combat the State, in order to overthrow the government; insulting the Iranian authorities; and propagating falsehoods in order to agitate the public mind and government officials with the intent of conveying the State as inefficient.

On May 8, 2003, the Court announced the sentence: Hossein Rafiee was sentenced to four years in prison with charges of "membership and activity in the *Melli-Mazhabi* illegal Coalition" and "Spreading propaganda against the State." The other charges were dropped, due to a lack of sufficient evidence.

On February 10, 2004, following an appeal by Hossein Rafiee's lawyer, the Court upheld the charges but reduced the prison term to three years.

This verdict was not implemented until 2015.

*Thursday, 16 June, 2016*

Dear Baba Hossein,

I haven't written a letter for years! Do people write letters anymore? In the age of emails, text messages, and social media, it's kind of weird to write a letter, isn't it? However, I have no choice but to write you a letter, as you don't have access to the internet or any kind of digital communication at the moment.

Today is the anniversary of your arrest. A year ago today, I woke up, made my breakfast, and started checking my emails and Facebook during breakfast, like other days. But something was not normal. I had gotten many messages with a common question: "Has your father been arrested?"

It was 9:00 in the morning in Canada and 5:30 in the evening in Iran. I called Maman.

"Has Baba been arrested?" I asked, without saying hello.

"Yes, in the morning. I just came back from the Evin prosecution center," she said.

I was the last one to find out! You know what is the most hateful thing about immigration? The time difference with your hometown. When the sun rises here, you are watching the sunset on the other side of the world. I'm always the last one to hear the news.

When I was asleep, you were being chased in the street like a criminal, like a thief! Your car was pulled over, you were taken out of the car by force, and you were brought to the Evin Prison without any explanation and without presenting you any arrest warrant. When I was asleep, you called Maman and told her to go to the Evin prosecution center. She went to you and you met each other for the last time. They detained you and Maman came back home alone.

Maman was telling me these stories on the phone and I was asking myself, *why wasn't I there?* I couldn't follow her words.

"Can you tell Mohammad?" she asked.

"Yes. Sure," I said and hung up the phone.

I wished I hadn't said that. How could I tell him? Next month will be his wedding party and, two months later, he will defend his PhD thesis. We were all supposed to go to the Netherlands and celebrate these two big events of his life together. How could I tell him that you won't be there? How, Baba? How?

Since the day of the raid, we have all been expecting your arrest. We've never talked about that day. Why, Baba? I don't know. Maybe we tried to forget it. I wish I could remove it from my memory, but no chance.

On the 30th of June, 2014, ten or more Intelligence agents raided our home, as if they expected to find a dangerous terrorist hiding there. They searched everywhere, perhaps to find shipments of arms and intelligence documents, but they found nothing, except your books and writings.

They confiscated all your writings, books, notes, computer hard drives, and also Maman's writings and her laptop. But I didn't want to give my laptop to them. Do you recall how tightly I held it in my arms?

It was a week before my immigration to Canada. I had saved all my memories in that laptop. Photos, videos, diaries, articles, projects... all my thirty years of life were preserved in that laptop. I didn't want to give it to them.

I was standing in a corner of the living room, holding my laptop and shouting at them, "I won't give it to you. This is mine. Get out of our home."

I was not shouting because of a damn laptop. No, not at all. It was because of this sudden raid of our privacy; because of searching our home, our bedrooms, and our drawers; because of their disrespectful behavior to you and Maman. I was shouting because they wanted to take my laptop and look at all my personal and private photos and diaries. Why? I didn't do anything wrong!

You know what was my real feeling in those moments? I felt my privacy was being violated and I wasn't able to do anything.

I had a lump in my throat that prevented me from shouting loudly. The more I tried, the more I felt I was choking. In a moment, I could neither shout nor breathe. I felt like my shouts and the lump closed up the airway in my throat. Do you recall that moment?

I sat on the sofa, pressing the laptop firmly against my chest. I preferred to die rather than leave the laptop. I remember your face. You had panicked and tried to tell me something, but I couldn't hear you. I was gasping for air and it felt like breathing through the tiniest tubes. I don't know how long it lasted, maybe ten seconds! But for me, it was long enough to review whole my life.

I wanted to show them that I wasn't scared of them, and truly, I wasn't. They talked to me, threatened me, and yelled at me, but I was sitting on the sofa, hugging the laptop as if it was the last thing left for me in life.

They warned you, "If you don't take the laptop from your daughter, we will use an electrical shocker."

You didn't want to force me. You never did. You've always taken the right side. And this time, you did the same. You told them, "This is my daughter's laptop. You are here for me. You don't have the right to take hers."

But they didn't care. They wanted to show their power. They attacked me, hit me, and took the laptop. I could never forget your face in those moments. I saw the pain and distress in your eyes that tried to tell me, "I'm sorry, darling, that I'm not able to do anything."

Two years has passed from that day, but I still have nightmares of those moments. They never go, Baba! They never go.

The intelligence agents left our home carrying our possessions, as if they belonged to them from the beginning. I was looking at my wounded and bruised arms, thinking why has this happened? What had you done that they were so furious at you?

It had been a while that you were writing articles about the nuclear deal. You were supporting the new government's diplomatic approach to resolving the nuclear problem with the world powers. You were supporting a deal that would end sanctions and remove the shadow of war from the country. But why had all these peaceful attitudes made them angry?

Maybe because you've believed that a sustainable future for the country would only be achieved through the release of political prisoners, free and fair elections, and an improvement of the human rights situation. Obviously, you had passed the red lines of the hardliners and they wanted to silence you.

Baba, do you remember our last goodbye at the airport? There were three of us: Maman, you and me. We arrived too soon, and to kill the time, we were taking selfies and photos. We were teasing Maman! She wanted to take a photo of us, but her hands were shaking and blurred all the photos.

At last, we didn't have a clear photo! The best one was you and me sitting on the airport benches as you put your arm around my shoulder. When I miss you terribly, I look at this blurred photo for hours and hours. It talks to me!

I left you and Maman alone, while I knew big adventures were waiting for you in the future. I came to a new land to rebuild my life, but as you know, just my body is here. I left my soul behind in that damn airport when I said goodbye to you. I still feel lost in this cold land! And I miss you so, so, so much.

Over the next months after my immigration, despite your on-going trial, I felt calmer. After each trial session, we talked on Skype, and it seemed everything was going fine. It was the calm before the storm!

Finally, in May, 2015, you were sentenced to six years in prison with the same accusations as fifteen years ago. And a month later, while you were waiting for your appeal, they arrested you. Again, they violated your right to freedom of speech. History was repeating itself in front of my eyes!

You had been arrested and I knew I should tell this to Mohammad before he read it in the news.

I called him and told him what had happened. He didn't say anything. Not even a word! You know him. He always keeps everything inside himself.

He had tried hard during the last months to set his wedding and his thesis defense dates close together so that we could stay the whole summer in Amsterdam and celebrate them together. And then, everything had suddenly been ruined. Why? Because some people didn't like your point of view, didn't tolerate your criticisms, and didn't give you the right to speak against their opinions!

After hanging up the phone, I stared at the trees outside the window for a long time. I don't remember what I was thinking about. Maybe I just wanted to disconnect from reality. I was thousands of miles away from you. What could I do for you? For Maman? For Mohammad?

Mohammad got married and you weren't there. He defended his PhD thesis and you weren't there, either. It was tough.

I don't have a child, but I can imagine how parents feel about their children. They enjoy seeing the growth of their children, they want to be part of all the important happenings of their life, like hearing the first word, watching the first step, and attending their graduation and marriage. Children also want their parents at their happy events to use the opportunity to honor them and to thank them for all they've done for them.

However, you and Mohammad were deprived from the most important events of his life. I don't know how you tolerated this, but if you ask how we tolerated it, I shall say it was very hard. We all had a lump in our throats during the ceremonies. We smiled at each other and the others, but deep down, nobody knew what we felt!

You were terribly missed at two specific moments, Baba. I have no words to describe my feelings, then.

The first moment was when Mohammad and Mahsa exchanged their vows and the officiant declared them husband and wife. Maman burst into tears and left the room. I tried to hold my tears back as my lips and hands were shaking. I hid myself behind other people so that Mohammad couldn't see my distress in the happiest moment of his life. Happiest moment of his life?! Our groom had a pale smile on his lips and no light in his eyes in the happiest moment of his life!

The second moment was right after his thesis defense when his supervisor, on behalf of the other opponents, came close to him, gave him his doctorate diploma, and declared him Dr. Mohammad Rafiee. It was such an honorable moment. You should have been there and seen this!

I took lots of photos and films for you, although none of them would compensate for the lost moments. Can you believe I haven't even looked at them once since taking them? It would just reopen my wounds! Maybe, one day, we can look at them together. I'll describe the moments and you can try to imagine them. Maybe one day, we can do this, Baba! Maybe one day.

I spent all of last summer with Maman and Mohammad. Maman was worried about you all the time. She thought if she was in Iran, she could do something to release you. But we all know that this time is different. This time, they intend to keep you in prison. They want to humiliate you and deprive you of all your rights.

When Maman told me for the first time that you are imprisoned in the same ward with pirates, I was shocked. "What? Pirates?" I couldn't believe her. But that was the truth. You've been imprisoned along with pirates of the Arabian Sea, drug traffickers, and prisoners of financial crimes! So humiliating!

You know what was the most annoying thing for me about your situation is? That you didn't have a bed for two months! Every night, when I went to my bed, I slept with this thought: "Where has Baba slept tonight?"

Once, you told me on the phone that those prisoners without beds are sleeping on the floor of the corridors and mosque of the prison, wherever they could find a spot. "We are sleeping packed like sardines!" you said, the best description you could have given me to imagine your situation at night. However, I still believe my imagination is more than what you've experienced.

It's been so painful to hear about your inhumane situation in prison. It is not just because you are my beloved father, but because this treatment is not fair to you, as a person who has served his country so much!

You had been a university professor for thirty years, and now you are in this situation. You don't have access to your necessary medical care, and you don't even have the right to use your legal monthly three-day furlough, like other prisoners. This really hurts when embezzlers, thieves, and drug traffickers have furloughs without any problem, but you, as a scholar, don't. Apparently, you are a more dangerous and threatening person than real criminals!!!

It is ridiculous that you have to bear all this pressure just because of your thoughts and opinions. If a scholar like you doesn't have the freedom to talk and write about his opinions, if a political activist like you doesn't have the freedom to criticize, and if a responsible citizen like you doesn't have the freedom to demand his rights, who would?

You know, Baba, if you lived here, in Canada, you would probably be busy now with research at a university, or writing your articles and books comfortably in a cozy room. And nobody would insult you, let alone imprison you.

Today is the anniversary of your arrest! Three hundred and sixty-five days have passed and there are still five more years to go and no sign of your release. I experienced the hardest time of my life during last year, from the challenges of immigration to your imprisonment to Maman's difficulties; these have broken me apart several times. But, every time, I compose myself to be stronger when I see that many people around the world care about you.

You can't imagine how many letters and articles have been written about you and how many petitions have been signed for you since your detention! I wished you could read these letters and see how the world is supporting you.

The American Chemical Society, Scholars at Risk, Committee of Concerned Scientists, the Middle East Studies Association's Committee on Academic Freedom, many science academies around the world, and hundreds of scholars, scientists, and Nobel laureates have written public and private letters to Iranian authorities demanding your release and asking them to observe your human rights and right to freedom of expression.

For the New Year, the students at Roger Williams University in the United States sent hundreds of postcards to the Evin Prison, although you never received them! They might have been lost somewhere on the way or, more likely, the authorities at the prison didn't give them to you.

Did you expect that much attention and support? I didn't. I'm speechless in front of them. The majority of these people don't know you, have never read your writings, and have never listened to your speeches, but they believe that you should have freedom of speech.

You know, after all these international protests to your arrest, deep down in my heart, I had hope that something good would happen at the Appeal Court in January, 2016. I thought the judge of the appeal would annul the previous verdict and order your release. Not only did this not happen, but we faced something worse!

On the appeal day, they didn't take you to the Court from prison! They didn't give you a chance to defend yourself against all those false accusations. And the judge held the Court without your presence, as if you basically didn't have a right to be there! This was so tyrannical and unjust!

Your appeal was upheld and I believe now your absence or presence in that Court has no effect on the final verdict. They had decided that before the appeal date!

I shouldn't get my hopes up. I was disappointed! I hurt a lot! Specifically, as it happened at the same time with the decline in Maman's health. She was diagnosed with a kidney stone and toxic nodular goiter within a week. I had hope that you might be released and be with her, but it didn't happen.

I was feeling lots of pressure on my shoulders and I could neither hold it nor release it. I was in a big dilemma; go back to Iran or do not?!

Maman was sick and needed someone to take care of her, and none of us were there. This was not fair to her! She insisted that Mohammad and I not go back to Iran. That's how mothers are, though; they sacrifice themselves for their children, but never want their children to do the same for them! She was afraid that Mohammad and I would be arrested or banned from the country because of talking about you in the media.

She told me, once, "If you come back, I will never forgive you!" I agreed not to go, despite my willingness to, and I still don't know if I did the right thing or not!

Everything was repeating! You were in prison again and Maman needed a surgery. My bitter memories of your previous detention were resurrected and I felt I was at the end of my rope!

I was crying at night and asking myself, "Why me? Why isn't my life normal?" I wished I had been born in a normal family. I wished I had never lived with the fear of your arrest and detention, with the fear of being watched and listened to in my private moments, with the fear of a raid of our house throughout my life. I was literally mad at you that my life had been overshadowed by your activities.

Don't be upset, Baba! You know how much I love you and am proud of you. I was just very exhausted and overwhelmed at that time.

Do you believe in miracles? I do.

A miracle happened to Maman. She was preparing herself for a surgery to remove her thyroid, when suddenly, in her last examination before the surgery, everything went back to normal! The miracle happened.

When I heard this, I prostrated, thanking God. I was crying and talking to him for hours. I had forgotten him, but he never does. His miracle showed me that I should have more faith in him. I'm sure he will change everything to a better situation in its proper time. I believe in this and I feel so much calmer, now.

Baba, it's the anniversary of your arrest and I haven't seen you for a year. I miss you so much. Maman told me, once, after meeting you in prison, that your grey hair all changed to white! I teased her that "Baba is bald, which hair do you mean?"

She said, "No, he still has some hair!" And we laughed.

You are getting old, huh? You were in prison for your seventy-second birthday. Did you hold a party with your cellmates? I don't think so. You've never been into birthday parties! However, this year, many people around the world held several birthday parties for you and created a witterstorm for your freedom on your birthday. I made a video clip of the photos and videos that people sent to me. It's your birthday gift. One day, I will give it to you.

Baba, they have the power to raid your home without any explanation and evidence, to hold private trials without your presence and sentence you without giving you any opportunity to defend yourself, to chase you in the street and arrest you without any warrant, and to imprison you in a place with prisoners who have contagious diseases, such as AIDS and Hepatitis, where you are bitten by bedbugs every night, where you have to take turns to use toilet, where you take showers with cold water, where you don't have access to internet, where you can't socialize with your fellows, where you don't have access to the medical care you need, where you can't eat, sleep, and live comfortably.

They have the power to deprive you from your inalienable rights, but they cannot change your thoughts. Despite all this torturous treatment of you, they haven't had the power to stop you from thinking and writing.

The day that our house was raided, you hugged me tightly in your arms after the agents left and whispered in my ear that you would answer their action, but not in their way; with your pen. "The pen is mightier than the sword," you said.

After a year of your detention, I'm writing this letter to tell you that you've already won. They haven't been able to silence you after a year of harsh and humiliating treatment. Your articles and letters from prison prove this.

Baba, I am so proud of you. These tough years will pass and you will be released with honor.

Be strong, be patient, and firmly stand your ground.

Love you so much.

On August 10, 2016, Hossein Rafiee transferred from prison to the hospital, as his health condition was declining.

On September 15, 2016, Hossein Rafiee was granted a medical furlough and released on bail after a surgery in the hospital and the necessity for more treatment.

On June 11 and September 28, 2017, by demand of a prosecutor, two medical commissions were held to examine the health situation of Hossein Rafiee. Both commissions verified that he cannot tolerate the prison conditions in his current health.

Hossein Rafiee is still free on bail. He is waiting for the appeal court that will be held based on the comments of the medical commissions.

*Friday, 23 February, 2018*
*Damavand*


My dear Anna,

I wanted to write this letter since I've heard that the letters you wrote to me during my imprisonment are going to be published as a book. I've always asked you to let other people read those letters because I've believed they are precious documents in the resistance to injustice and struggles against oppression. I am happy that you finally decided to publish them.

I remember very well how proud I was of you when I read the letters for the first time after I was released from prison. My little girl had reached a level of moral and social maturity where she was able to defend human rights and reveal oppression by writing about and documenting these events. I was filled with joy and hope. These feelings were not just because you are my daughter —although that doubled my happiness— but mainly because a seventeen-year-old girl was part of human development and reform in society, and such things cannot be achieved except through protests and fighting against the lawbreakers and violators of human rights.

I was grateful that you had shared your feelings with no filter and that you wrote about your fears, angers, anxieties, and all the difficulties, even though my heart ached so badly knowing what you had been through at that age.

Your letters were like a miracle which brought me back to the life I had lost after six months' detention in solitary confinement. The more I read, the more I wanted to know what happened during my absence. And you had done a wonderful job by describing everything in detail. I witnessed your growth and maturity through the lines of the letters as if years had passed instead of six months.

I have to confess something. Your letters motivated me to write my book, *Legal Subversion*. I told myself, "If my seventeen-year-old daughter could use her voice and expose oppression with her pen, then I could do the same even more." And I wrote that book in defense of myself and as a response to what I was wrongfully accused of.

Thank you, my darling, for being an inspiration.

Anna,

You live now in a developed country and enjoy the benefits that this brings. But you must keep in mind that developed countries have not been – and won't be – built without struggles and sacrifices.

The Iranian Revolution, as a result of years of struggles and protests, happened in 1979 to achieve independence, justice, and freedom, like other developed countries. However, it soon became clear that there were serious obstacles for actualizing the revolutionaries' aspirations. Since then, my friends and I have tried to take steps toward those aspirations, but unfortunately, we've faced problems and obstacles, some of which are reflected in your letters.

In 2001, when I was released from prison, it was hard for me to predict the future of the country. I didn't know whether reformism would succeed or whether those who sought hegemony would cause society to collapse. But I was sure of one thing: that reforming the country is the correct path toward democracy.

Back then, there were few of us on this path, but over the last two decades we've been growing in number and now we are many, in number and ideologies. And I am glad that you are still one of those fighters.

I've always known that there is a strong will, growing power, pure intention, and a sense of humanitarian duty in you that would lead you to confront injustice, the violation of human rights, and the denial of freedoms. You showed this to me more than ever when I was imprisoned again in 2015. You bravely used your voice to defend my rights and it was because of your effort that I received worldwide support, which I didn't expect for myself.

I told myself in prison, "Why should I be worried for the future? The next generation has risen to continue on the path toward democracy and freedom." Lots of young people – like you – have demanded their rights and they have no fear of confronting tyranny; the world has heard the sound of their protests, has seen their will for change, and has given warm responses to their courage.

One example of such responses includes the hundreds of letters and petitions sent to Iranian authorities demanding my release from prison. All of their actions remind me of this poem by Sa'adi Shirazi, who said in the 13th century:

*Human beings are members of a whole,*
*In creation of one essence and soul.*
*If one member is afflicted with pain,*
*Other members uneasy will remain.*

My dear Anna,

I have no doubt that you are bright enough to find your own path and make your own choices, but let me share an experience with you as a father in his mid-seventies, whose life is threatened with natural various diseases and unnatural (harsh conditions in prison) causes.

You still have forty years to reach my current age. In these years the world will change more than it has changed during the last four decades. Many rulers will come and many others will be gone. Some like Mosaddegh, Gandhi, Mandela, and Allende will strive for human development and some like Hitler, Saddam Hossein, the Taliban, and Daesh will inflict genocide and crimes against humanity. But always remember: what will last is humanity.

Humanity has no boundary, no religion, no color, no belief, no gender, no nationality, and no ideology. The future of humanity will be made by people like Martin Luther King, Tutu, and Mother Teresa. Those with good intentions and actions will be the ones to make progress for humanity, not the rulers who are captivated by their power and egoism.

No improvement can be achieved in society without the process of confrontation and reconciliation: confronting injustice and reconciliation with the recognition of the diversity of human thoughts. And I hope that you live your life in this process. Confront any falsehood and respect diversity in religion, thought, race, belief, and so on.

You live now in a society that violated the rights of indigenous people in the early years of its establishment and foundation, but has now recognized democracy and human rights and provides for human development. I wish that with your knowledge of western experience, you can help to improve Iranian society and the other societies which need help and support.

Keep sharing your experiences with others, as you've already done by publishing your letters, and more than that, read others' experiences. This is how we could grow together.

And please never lose your soulful mind and your compassionate heart.

With love,
Baba Hossein